Leading with Purpose: Building High-Performing Teams

Linda Thornton

Published by DMG Ltd.
© 2024

Leading with Purpose: Building High Performance Teams

Contents

Chapter 1: Understanding Purpose in Leadership 6
Defining Purpose in a Team Context   6
The Role of Purpose in Behavior Modification   9
Aligning Team Goals with Organizational Purpose   11

Chapter 2: Managing Tasks, Not People 16
The Shift from People Management to Task Management   16
Strategies for Effective Task Delegation.   19
Building a Task-Oriented Culture   22

Chapter 3: Disciplining Behaviors, Not People 27
Understanding Behavioral Discipline   27
Techniques for Modifying Unproductive Behaviors   30
Creating a Positive Environment for Behavioral Change   33

Chapter 4: Behavior Modification Techniques in the Workplace 37
Overview of Behavior Modification Strategies   37
Implementing Positive Reinforcement   40
Utilizing Consequences for Behavioral Change   43

Chapter 5: Leadership Approaches Focused on Task Orientation .. 47
Task Oriented Leadership Styles   47
Balancing Task Orientation with Team Dynamics   50
Case Studies of Successful Task- Oriented Leaders   53

Chapter 6: Employee Engagement Through Task Ownership 57
The Importance of Task Ownership   57
Strategies to Foster Engagement and Ownership   60
Measuring the Impact of Task Ownership on Performance   63

Chapter 7: Behavioral Coaching for Enhanced Team Performance 67
The Role of Coaching in Behavior Modification   67
Techniques for Effective Behavioral Coaching   70
Setting Coaching Goals for Team Performance   73

Chapter 8: Performance Metrics for Task-Based Assessments 77
Identifying Key Performance Indicators ... 77
Designing Task-Based Assessment Tools ... 80
Analyzing Performance Data for Continuous Improvement ... 83

Chapter 9: Creating a Sustainable Culture of High Performance 87
Embedding Purpose into Team Culture ... 87
Strategies for Sustaining High Performance ... 90
Future Trends in Team Leadership and Behavior Modification ... 93

Chapter 10: Conclusion: Leading with Purpose 97
Recap of Key Concepts ... 97
The Future of Purpose-Driven Leadership ... 100
Call to Action for Managers and Leaders ... 103

Chapter 11: Quick Decision- Making Frameworks 108
The Importance of Swift Decisions ... 108
The 4D Decision Model ... 111
Utilizing the Eisenhower Matrix ... 113
The 5-Second Rule for Timely Choices ... 116

Chapter 12: Instant Conflict Resolution Tactics 120
Understanding Conflict Dynamics ... 120
The DESC Model for Effective Communication ... 124
Quick Mediation Techniques ... 126
Implementing Win-Win Solutions ... 129

Chapter 13: Rapid Goal Setting and Prioritization 134
SMART Goals in a Nutshell ... 134
The 1-Page Goal Setting Worksheet ... 136
Prioritizing with the ABCD Method ... 139
Aligning Team Goals with Organizational Objectives ... 143

Chapter 14: Rapid Coaching Techniques 147
The Power of Brief Coaching Sessions ... 147
The GROW Model for Instant Guidance ... 150
Effective Questioning Techniques ... 152

Celebrating Small Wins	155
Chapter 15: Efficient Performance Feedback Methods	**159**
Delivering Feedback in Under a Minute	159
The Sandwich Method Explained	161
Utilizing Peer Feedback for Growth	164
Creating a Feedback Culture	167
Chapter 16: Simple Change Management Approaches	**172**
The Need for Change in Business	172
The ADKAR Model Simplified	175
Communicating Change Effectively	178
Engaging Teams in the Change Process	181

Chapter 1: Understanding Purpose in Leadership

Defining Purpose in a Team Context

Defining purpose in a team context is essential for managers and leaders who seek to cultivate high-performing teams. Purpose provides a clear direction and serves as a motivational force that aligns individual efforts with the overarching goals of the organization. When teams understand their purpose, they are more likely to exhibit behaviors that contribute to collective success rather than merely focusing on individual tasks. This alignment fosters a culture of accountability and engagement, where team members take ownership of their roles and are committed to achieving shared objectives.

In a task-oriented leadership approach, defining purpose requires a deliberate focus on the tasks at hand while contextualizing them within the larger framework of the organization's mission and vision. Managers can facilitate this by clearly communicating how specific tasks contribute to broader goals. This not only enhances clarity but also empowers team members to see the significance of their roles. By framing tasks within a purposeful context, leaders can encourage a sense of belonging and commitment among team members, leading to improved performance outcomes.

Behavior modification techniques play a crucial role in reinforcing purpose within teams. Leaders can implement strategies that acknowledge and reward behaviors aligned with the team's purpose, thereby fostering a culture that prioritizes task completion and collaboration. For instance, recognizing team efforts that exemplify commitment to purpose can motivate employees to replicate those behaviors. Additionally, constructive feedback can guide team members in adjusting behaviors that may detract from achieving the group's objectives, ensuring that the focus remains on collective success rather than individual shortcomings.

Employee engagement is significantly enhanced when individuals feel a sense of ownership over their tasks. Leaders can cultivate this ownership by involving team members in the process of defining purpose. This collaborative approach not only empowers employees but also allows them to contribute their insights and perspectives, which can enrich the team's overall purpose.

When team members actively participate in shaping their purpose, they are more likely to embrace their responsibilities and hold themselves accountable for their performance, leading to higher levels of engagement and productivity.

Finally, performance metrics should align with the defined purpose to create a clear pathway for assessment and improvement. Task-based assessments that reflect the team's objectives can provide valuable insights into performance levels and areas for development. By utilizing metrics that measure both individual contributions and team outcomes, leaders can more effectively coach their teams toward achieving their defined purpose. This data-driven approach allows managers to identify patterns in behavior and performance, enabling them to tailor their leadership strategies to enhance overall team effectiveness while reinforcing the intrinsic value of purpose in their work.

The Role of Purpose in Behavior Modification

The role of purpose in behavior modification within high-performing teams is crucial for fostering an environment where tasks are managed effectively and employee engagement is maximized. A clear sense of purpose not only guides individuals in understanding their roles but also aligns their behaviors with organizational goals. When managers articulate a compelling purpose, it serves as a motivational force that drives team members to engage more deeply with their tasks. This clarity helps in reducing distractions and enhances focus, allowing employees to see the impact of their contributions on broader objectives.

Purpose acts as a framework within which behavior modification techniques can be effectively applied. By establishing a strong organizational vision, leaders can implement strategies that align with this vision while addressing specific behaviors that need adjustment. For instance, when teams understand how their tasks contribute to the overall mission, they are more likely to embrace feedback and adapt their behaviors accordingly. This alignment fosters a culture of accountability, where employees take ownership of their actions and are motivated to refine their performance in pursuit of shared goals.

Behavioral coaching emerges as a vital tool in this context, providing tailored support that reinforces the connection between purpose and individual performance. Managers who engage in coaching conversations can help team members identify their personal motivations and align them with the team's objectives. This individualized approach not only enhances performance but also deepens employee engagement, as individuals feel seen and valued in their roles. The more leaders invest in understanding their teams' aspirations, the more effectively they can guide behavior modification that resonates on a personal level.

Furthermore, performance metrics play a significant role in reinforcing purpose-driven behavior modification. By establishing clear, measurable outcomes linked to the organizational purpose, leaders can create a transparent system that tracks progress and celebrates achievements. This data-driven approach allows for ongoing adjustments in strategies and behaviors, ensuring that team members remain focused on the tasks that drive success. Regularly reviewing these metrics in relation to purpose fosters a sense of shared ownership, motivating employees to commit to continuous improvement.

Ultimately, the integration of purpose into behavior modification strategies cultivates a high-performing team culture where tasks are managed rather than people. By emphasizing discipline of behaviors instead of individuals, managers can create an environment that encourages growth, accountability, and collaboration. In this way, purpose not only shapes individual behaviors but also strengthens the collective performance of the team, leading to sustainable success and a more engaged workforce.

Aligning Team Goals with Organizational Purpose

Aligning team goals with organizational purpose is essential for fostering a cohesive and high-performing environment. When team objectives mirror the overarching goals of the organization, it creates a sense of unity and direction among team members.

Managers and leaders play a pivotal role in this alignment, as they must ensure that every member understands how their contributions fit into the larger picture. This alignment not only enhances productivity but also fosters employee engagement, as individuals see the significance of their roles within the context of the organization's mission.

To effectively align team goals with organizational purpose, it is crucial to begin with a clear understanding of that purpose. Leaders should communicate the organization's vision and mission in a way that resonates with team members. This involves breaking down the strategic goals of the organization into tangible objectives that teams can work towards. By translating high- level aspirations into specific, actionable targets, managers can create a roadmap that guides teams toward achieving collective success while remaining aligned with the broader organizational objectives.

Behavior modification techniques can be instrumental in this alignment process. By focusing on specific behaviors that contribute to team goals, leaders can reinforce positive actions and redirect any that do not serve the organizational purpose. For instance, implementing regular feedback mechanisms can help team members understand how their behaviors impact their performance and the team's success. This could include using performance metrics that not only track task completion but also evaluate the quality and effectiveness of the behaviors exhibited by team members.

Furthermore, fostering a culture of task ownership is vital for aligning individual goals with the organization's purpose. When employees take ownership of their tasks, they are more likely to feel a sense of responsibility towards achieving the team's objectives.

Leaders can encourage this ownership by providing autonomy in decision-making and recognizing individual contributions to the team's success. This empowerment not only increases engagement but also cultivates a proactive attitude among team members, leading to enhanced performance and innovation.

Finally, behavioral coaching serves as a powerful tool for leaders seeking to align team goals with organizational purpose. By adopting a coaching approach, managers can facilitate open dialogues about performance expectations and personal growth. This ongoing support helps team members navigate challenges and reinforces their commitment to the team's objectives.

Additionally, regular assessments of performance metrics can aid in identifying areas for improvement and celebrating achievements. This continuous feedback loop not only nurtures individual growth but also strengthens the collective focus on the organizational purpose, leading to sustained high performance.

Chapter 2: Managing Tasks, Not People

The Shift from People Management to Task Management

The transition from traditional people management to a focus on task management marks a significant evolution in leadership strategies. Historically, management styles emphasized the oversight and development of employees as individuals, often leading to a more subjective approach to performance evaluation. However, the increasing complexity of workplace dynamics and the demand for agility in achieving results have prompted a shift toward managing tasks rather than directly overseeing people. This paradigm shift allows managers to foster a more results-oriented environment that empowers teams to take ownership of their responsibilities, ultimately driving performance and engagement.

At the core of task management is the recognition that behaviors, rather than personalities, are what influence team dynamics and outcomes. By disciplining behaviors instead of targeting individuals, leaders can create a culture where feedback is constructive and focused on improvement.

This approach not only enhances accountability but also encourages employees to embrace a mindset of continuous development. Managers can implement behavior modification techniques that align with organizational goals, providing clear guidelines for expected outcomes while allowing team members the autonomy to navigate their paths to success.

Leadership approaches that emphasize task orientation streamline processes and clarify expectations. By defining tasks with precision, leaders can minimize ambiguity and ensure that all team members understand their roles within the larger context of the organization's objectives. This clarity not only enhances productivity but also fosters a sense of purpose among employees, as they see how their contributions directly impact the team's success. Task-oriented leadership encourages collaboration, as team members work together to achieve shared goals, reinforcing a collective commitment to performance excellence.

Engaging employees through task ownership is another crucial aspect of this shift. When individuals are given the responsibility to manage their own tasks, they are more likely to feel invested in their work. This sense of ownership fosters intrinsic motivation, as team members recognize the significance of their contributions. By encouraging autonomy in task management, leaders can cultivate a workforce that is not only engaged but also more innovative, as employees take initiative to find solutions and improve processes. This empowerment leads to a more dynamic workplace where creativity and efficiency thrive.

To effectively assess team performance in this new paradigm, leaders must develop performance metrics that reflect task-based assessments. These metrics should focus on outcomes related to task completion, quality of work, and adherence to timelines rather than subjective evaluations of individual effort. By adopting clear and objective criteria for success, managers can track progress more accurately and provide targeted feedback that drives further improvement. This data-driven approach not only enhances accountability but also enables leaders to identify high performers and areas for development, ultimately leading to a more cohesive and high-performing team.

Strategies for Effective Task Delegation.

Effective task delegation is a critical component of successful leadership. Managers and leaders must recognize that the ability to assign tasks appropriately can significantly influence team dynamics and overall performance. The first strategy for effective task delegation is to clearly define the tasks at hand. This involves breaking down larger projects into manageable components, detailing the objectives and expected outcomes. By articulating the specifics of each task, leaders ensure that team members understand their responsibilities and the importance of their contributions, fostering a sense of ownership and engagement.

Another essential strategy is to assess the strengths and weaknesses of team members.

Understanding individual capabilities allows leaders to delegate tasks based on skill sets and interests. This alignment not only enhances the likelihood of success but also increases employee satisfaction and motivation. When team members feel that their unique talents are being utilized, they are more likely to take ownership of their tasks, leading to higher levels of engagement and performance. Additionally, this approach encourages professional growth, as team members are challenged and supported in developing new skills.

Communication plays a vital role in the task delegation process. Leaders should establish open lines of communication, providing team members with the opportunity to ask questions and seek clarification on assigned tasks. Regular check-ins and feedback sessions can help maintain alignment and address any challenges that arise. This ongoing dialogue not only reinforces expectations but also fosters a culture of collaboration and trust. By creating an environment where team members feel comfortable discussing their progress and obstacles, leaders can effectively support their efforts and ensure that tasks are completed to the best of their abilities.

Monitoring and evaluating performance metrics is crucial in assessing the effectiveness of task delegation. Leaders should implement clear performance indicators that align with organizational goals and the specific objectives of each task. By tracking progress and outcomes, managers can identify areas for improvement and provide targeted behavioral coaching to enhance team performance. This data-driven approach not only informs future delegation decisions but also highlights successes, reinforcing positive behaviors that contribute to high-performing teams.

Finally, encouraging a culture of accountability is essential for effective task delegation.

Leaders must hold team members responsible for their assigned tasks while also supporting them in overcoming challenges. This balance of accountability and support fosters a sense of ownership and commitment to tasks, ultimately driving team performance. By recognizing and rewarding accomplishments, leaders can motivate their teams and reinforce the importance of task-based engagement. In doing so, they cultivate an environment where team members are empowered to take initiative and contribute meaningfully to organizational success.

Building a Task-Oriented Culture

Building a task-oriented culture within an organization is essential for fostering high-performance teams and achieving strategic objectives. This approach emphasizes the management of tasks rather than the individuals who perform them, creating an environment where behaviors are adjusted to enhance productivity and morale. By focusing on what needs to be accomplished, leaders can disengage from the pitfalls of micromanagement and instead promote autonomy and accountability among team members. This shift not only clarifies expectations but also empowers employees to take ownership of their roles, leading to increased engagement and job satisfaction.

To effectively build a task-oriented culture, leaders must implement behavior modification techniques that encourage desired actions while providing constructive feedback. These techniques include setting clear, measurable goals that align with the company's objectives, ensuring that all team members understand their responsibilities. Regularly reviewing performance metrics related to task completion can help identify areas for improvement and reinforce positive behaviors. By establishing a framework for accountability, managers can create a culture where employees feel supported in their efforts to achieve targets and are motivated to excel.

Leadership approaches focused on task orientation foster a collaborative environment where team members can thrive. This involves training leaders to prioritize task alignment and to recognize the impact of their leadership style on team dynamics. Effective leaders model task-oriented behaviors themselves, demonstrating how prioritizing tasks leads to improved outcomes. They also promote open communication, allowing team members to discuss challenges related to their tasks and collaborate on solutions. This collaborative spirit not only enhances teamwork but also builds trust and respect among colleagues.

Employee engagement through task ownership is a

critical aspect of a task-oriented culture. When team members take ownership of their tasks, they are more likely to invest their energy and creativity into their work.

Encouraging this sense of ownership can be achieved through delegation and empowering employees to make decisions related to their tasks. By involving employees in the planning and execution of their work, leaders can cultivate a sense of pride and responsibility that drives performance. This engagement is further enhanced when employees see the direct impact of their contributions on team and organizational success.

Behavioral coaching is a valuable tool for enhancing team performance in a task-oriented culture. Leaders should actively engage in coaching to develop their team's skills and reinforce positive behaviors that contribute to task completion. This process involves providing timely feedback, recognizing achievements, and offering support for overcoming obstacles. By fostering a growth mindset within the team, leaders can encourage continuous improvement and innovation. Ultimately, a task-oriented culture built on these principles not only boosts productivity but also creates a more fulfilling and dynamic workplace for employees.

Chapter 3: Disciplining Behaviors, Not People

Understanding Behavioral Discipline

Understanding Behavioral Discipline is crucial for managers and leaders who aim to cultivate high-performing teams. Behavioral discipline focuses on modifying specific actions and habits rather than targeting individuals. This approach not only fosters a positive work environment but also promotes accountability among team members. By emphasizing behaviors, leaders can create a culture where employees feel empowered to take ownership of their tasks and responsibilities, ultimately leading to enhanced performance and engagement.

When leaders adopt a task-oriented mindset, they shift their focus from managing people to managing tasks. This involves recognizing that behaviors can be modified through systematic approaches rather than punitive measures.

Behavioral discipline encompasses various techniques that address both the antecedents and consequences of behaviors in the workplace. By implementing strategies such as positive reinforcement, setting clear expectations, and providing constructive feedback, managers can effectively guide their teams toward desired outcomes while maintaining a supportive atmosphere.

Behavior modification techniques play a pivotal role in shaping team dynamics. These techniques can include reward systems for task completion, regular check-ins to monitor progress, and the establishment of performance metrics that align with organizational goals. By measuring behaviors and outcomes, leaders can identify patterns that require intervention and celebrate successes that reinforce positive behaviors.

This data-driven approach not only clarifies expectations but also motivates employees to engage more deeply with their work, fostering a culture of continuous improvement.

Leadership approaches that focus on task

orientation also enhance employee engagement through task ownership. When team members feel a sense of ownership over their tasks, they are more likely to demonstrate commitment and initiative.

Leaders can encourage this ownership by providing autonomy in how tasks are completed while offering support and guidance when necessary. This balance allows employees to take pride in their work, which can lead to higher levels of satisfaction and reduced turnover rates, as individuals feel their contributions are valued.

Finally, behavioral coaching emerges as a vital tool for enhancing team performance. By applying coaching techniques, leaders can help employees identify areas for improvement and develop personalized action plans. Coaching conversations should be framed around specific behaviors and their impact on team dynamics and performance metrics. This ongoing dialogue not only fosters individual growth but also builds a cohesive team culture where everyone feels responsible for their contributions. As a result, managers can lead their teams with purpose, driving both individual and collective success through effective behavioral discipline.

Techniques for Modifying Unproductive Behaviors

In today's dynamic workplace, managers must focus on modifying unproductive behaviors to foster a culture of high performance. One effective technique is the use of positive reinforcement, which emphasizes recognizing and rewarding desirable behaviors rather than merely punishing undesirable ones. By acknowledging team members who demonstrate initiative, meet deadlines, or collaborate effectively, leaders create an environment where positive behaviors are encouraged and repeated. This approach not only uplifts morale but also reinforces the notion that productive behaviors contribute to team success and individual growth.

Another valuable technique is the establishment of clear expectations and goals. When team members understand what is expected of them, they are more likely to align their efforts with organizational objectives.

Leaders should work collaboratively with their teams to set measurable and attainable goals, ensuring that each member has ownership over their tasks. This alignment fosters accountability, as employees can clearly see how their contributions impact the team's overall performance. Furthermore, regular check-ins and feedback sessions can provide opportunities for leaders to address any deviations from expected behaviors promptly.

Behavioral coaching is a powerful method for modifying unproductive behaviors. Through one-on-one coaching sessions, managers can identify specific areas where an employee may struggle and provide tailored guidance to help them improve. This personalized approach not only addresses the root causes of unproductive behaviors but also empowers employees by equipping them with the skills and strategies needed for success. By focusing on development rather than discipline, leaders create a supportive atmosphere that encourages continuous improvement and fosters resilience within the team.

Incorporating performance metrics into the evaluation process is essential for task-based assessments. By establishing clear metrics related to individual and team performance, leaders can objectively measure progress and identify patterns of unproductive behaviors.

These metrics should be communicated transparently to the entire team, allowing employees to understand how their performance is evaluated. Utilizing data-driven insights enables managers to pinpoint specific behaviors that require modification, facilitating targeted interventions that lead to improved outcomes.

Lastly, cultivating a culture of open communication is critical for sustaining behavior modification efforts. Leaders should encourage team members to share their thoughts and experiences related to task performance, creating a safe space for dialogue. This transparency fosters trust and allows employees to voice concerns about obstacles they may face in maintaining productivity. When employees feel heard and supported, they are more likely to engage in self-reflection and take proactive steps to modify unproductive behaviors, ultimately leading to enhanced team performance and a more cohesive work environment.

Creating a Positive Environment for Behavioral Change

Creating a positive environment for behavioral change is essential in fostering high- performing teams. As managers and leaders, it is crucial to establish a workplace culture that encourages individuals to take ownership of their tasks and responsibilities. This culture must be rooted in the understanding that we manage tasks, not people. By focusing on the tasks at hand, leaders can create a framework that supports behavioral modification techniques designed to enhance performance. This approach not only empowers employees but also aligns their actions with the organization's goals, facilitating a conducive atmosphere for change.

To create this environment, leaders should prioritize clear communication and transparency. Employees need to understand the expectations tied to their tasks, as well as the rationale behind specific behavioral modifications. When leaders articulate their vision and the importance of behavioral change within the context of task completion, employees are more likely to engage with the process. This clarity provides a sense of purpose and direction, allowing team members to see how their individual contributions impact the larger organizational objectives. Effective communication also fosters trust, enabling employees to feel safe in expressing concerns or challenges they may face in adapting to new behaviors.

In addition to clear communication, it is vital to implement behavioral coaching techniques that focus on positive reinforcement.

Recognizing and rewarding employees for their efforts in adopting new behaviors can significantly enhance motivation and commitment. Leaders should celebrate small victories and provide constructive feedback that emphasizes growth rather than punishment. This shift in focus from disciplining individuals to addressing behaviors cultivates a supportive environment where team members feel valued. By reinforcing desired behaviors, leaders can drive sustained change and encourage a culture of continuous improvement.

Engagement is another critical factor in creating a positive environment for behavioral change. When employees feel a sense of ownership over their tasks, they are more likely to take initiative and actively participate in the behavioral modification process.

Managers should involve team members in setting performance metrics and defining success criteria, allowing them to take part in their development journey. This ownership not only increases accountability but also enhances the connection between individual performance and team success. As employees witness the impact of their contributions, they become more invested in the team's overall objectives and are more likely to embrace the necessary behavioral changes.

Finally, it is essential for leaders to model the behaviors they wish to see within their teams. By embodying the principles of task-oriented leadership and demonstrating a commitment to behavioral change, leaders set a powerful example for their team members. Consistency in actions and attitudes reinforces the importance of these behaviors and encourages employees to follow suit. When leaders actively participate in the process of behavioral modification and engage with their teams in meaningful ways, they create a ripple effect that fosters a culture of high performance. A positive environment for behavioral change, characterized by clear communication, behavioral coaching, engagement, and exemplary leadership, ultimately drives the success of high- performing teams.

Chapter 4: Behavior Modification Techniques in the Workplace

Overview of Behavior Modification Strategies

Behavior modification strategies are essential tools for managers and leaders aiming to cultivate high-performing teams. These strategies focus on altering specific behaviors rather than attempting to change individuals as a whole. By concentrating on behaviors linked to task performance, leaders can create an environment where employees feel empowered to take ownership of their roles.

This approach aligns with the philosophy of managing tasks instead of people, allowing for a more objective assessment of performance and fostering a culture of accountability and improvement.

One widely recognized behavior modification technique is positive reinforcement, which involves rewarding desired behaviors to encourage their recurrence. In the workplace, this can manifest as recognition programs, bonuses, or other incentives that acknowledge employees for achieving specific performance metrics. By reinforcing positive behaviors, leaders not only enhance employee engagement but also promote a culture where individuals are motivated to excel in their tasks. This method is particularly effective in task-oriented environments, where clear expectations and outcomes are crucial for success.

Another key strategy is the use of behavioral modeling, where leaders demonstrate the desired behaviors they wish to see in their teams. By embodying the standards of performance, managers can effectively communicate expectations and provide a tangible example for employees to follow. This form of leadership fosters a cooperative atmosphere, encouraging team members to emulate positive behaviors. Furthermore, it reinforces the concept that behaviors can be learned and modified, thus supporting the overall goal of behavior modification in the workplace.

Task-oriented leadership approaches often

incorporate the practice of setting clear, measurable performance metrics. These metrics serve as benchmarks for evaluating employee performance and behavior. By establishing specific goals, managers can guide their teams in understanding what is expected of them. Moreover, regular assessments against these metrics provide opportunities for feedback and adjustment, ensuring that employees can continuously improve their performance. This structured approach not only aids in behavior modification but also enhances overall team productivity.

Behavioral coaching is another important component of behavior modification strategies. This process involves personalized support and guidance aimed at helping employees develop the skills necessary to improve their performance. Through one-on- one coaching sessions, leaders can identify specific behavioral challenges and collaboratively create action plans to address them. This tailored approach not only boosts individual performance but also contributes to the overall effectiveness of the team. By focusing on behaviors rather than personal attributes, managers can facilitate a more constructive dialogue, ultimately leading to enhanced team performance and achievement of organizational goals.

Implementing Positive Reinforcement

Implementing positive reinforcement within a team environment is a powerful strategy for fostering a culture of high performance.

Positive reinforcement involves recognizing and rewarding desired behaviors, thereby encouraging their recurrence. In a task- oriented leadership approach, this method aligns seamlessly with the objective of managing tasks rather than individuals. By focusing on the specific behaviors that contribute to task completion, managers can create a dynamic where employees feel valued for their contributions, leading to increased engagement and motivation.

To effectively implement positive reinforcement, it is crucial for leaders to identify the key behaviors that drive task performance within their teams. This involves analyzing performance metrics to determine what specific actions lead to successful outcomes. By establishing clear expectations and openly communicating these to team members, leaders can create a roadmap for success. Recognizing and celebrating these behaviors, whether through verbal acknowledgment, rewards, or other incentives, reinforces the idea that employees are contributing to the team's goals, thus fostering a sense of ownership and pride in their work.

Behavioral coaching plays a significant role in the process of positive reinforcement.

Managers can engage in one-on-one coaching sessions focused on reinforcing specific behaviors that lead to task success. This approach not only helps employees understand how their actions impact overall team performance but also empowers them to take ownership of their tasks. By incorporating feedback into these coaching sessions, leaders can guide their teams toward continuous improvement, ensuring that the reinforcement is not only positive but also constructive in nature.

In addition to individual recognition, implementing positive reinforcement on a team level can amplify its effects. Leaders can create team-based incentives that encourage collaboration and collective achievement. This not only enhances the sense of community within the team but also aligns individual goals with team objectives. When team members see their peers being rewarded for positive behaviors, it creates a ripple effect that motivates others to strive for the same recognition, leading to a more cohesive and high-performing environment.

Finally, it is essential for leaders to regularly assess the effectiveness of their positive reinforcement strategies. By measuring performance metrics and gathering feedback from team members, managers can evaluate whether the reinforcement practices are achieving the desired outcomes. This ongoing assessment allows for adjustments to be made, ensuring that the approach remains relevant and impactful. In the ever-evolving landscape of workplace dynamics, leaders who prioritize positive reinforcement as a behavior modification technique will find themselves at the forefront of fostering engaged, high- performing teams.

Utilizing Consequences for Behavioral Change

Utilizing consequences effectively is a critical strategy for fostering behavioral change within high-performing teams. Managers and leaders who adopt a task-oriented approach understand that while they manage tasks, the behaviors that drive those tasks are paramount. By focusing on the consequences associated with specific behaviors, leaders can create an environment where positive behaviors are reinforced, and negative behaviors are addressed constructively. This shift in focus allows teams to operate more efficiently, as employees become more engaged in their tasks and aligned with organizational goals.

The concept of consequences in behavior modification is rooted in the principles of operant conditioning. Positive reinforcement, such as recognition or rewards, can enhance desirable behaviors and encourage employees to take ownership of their tasks. For instance, when a team member consistently meets deadlines or exceeds expectations, acknowledging their efforts publicly can motivate not only that individual but also their peers. By systematically applying consequences, leaders can cultivate a culture of accountability where employees feel empowered to contribute proactively to their teams.

Conversely, addressing undesirable behaviors through appropriate consequences is equally important. This does not entail punitive measures but rather constructive feedback that guides employees toward more effective behaviors. For example, if a team member frequently misses deadlines, a leader can engage in a discussion to identify underlying issues and collaboratively develop strategies to improve time management. This approach emphasizes discipline towards behaviors rather than the individual, reinforcing the notion that the goal is to enhance performance rather than punish shortcomings.

In addition to reinforcing positive behaviors and addressing negative ones, leaders must establish clear performance metrics that align with the desired outcomes. By defining what success looks like in terms of task completion and behavior, managers can provide specific feedback that helps employees understand how their actions impact team performance. This clarity not only drives accountability but also fosters a sense of ownership among team members, as they can see the direct correlation between their behaviors and the team's overall success.

Ultimately, effectively utilizing consequences for behavioral change requires intentionality and consistency. Leaders must be vigilant in monitoring behaviors and the associated outcomes, ensuring that the consequences are fair, timely, and aligned with organizational values. By fostering an environment where behaviors are regularly assessed and addressed, managers can lead their teams toward sustained high performance, transforming challenges into opportunities for growth and development.

Chapter 5: Leadership Approaches Focused on Task Orientation

Task-Oriented Leadership Styles

Task-oriented leadership styles focus primarily on the tasks at hand and the efficient completion of objectives, making them vital in environments where productivity and performance are paramount. Managers who adopt this approach prioritize defining roles, setting clear expectations, and establishing structured processes. This leadership style is particularly effective in organizations with well- defined goals and deadlines, where clarity and accountability can drive team performance. By concentrating on task completion, leaders can foster a sense of urgency and direction that often leads to heightened productivity and improved outcomes.

In task-oriented leadership, discipline is centered on behaviors that align with organizational goals rather than on personal attributes of team members. This method emphasizes addressing behaviors that hinder performance and rewarding those that contribute to task completion. Leaders can employ behavior modification techniques to reinforce positive behaviors, such as providing constructive feedback, recognizing achievements, and implementing corrective actions when necessary. This focus on behavior rather than personality helps create an environment where employees understand the expectations and can adjust their actions accordingly, leading to improved individual and team performance.

Another critical aspect of task-oriented leadership is the emphasis on performance metrics. Leaders must establish and communicate clear performance indicators that reflect the organization's objectives. By using quantifiable metrics, managers can objectively assess team and individual performance, which can lead to data-driven decisions regarding resource allocation and employee development. This approach not only helps in tracking progress but also motivates team members to take ownership of their tasks, as they can see the direct impact of their contributions on overall success.

Engagement within a task-oriented framework is significantly enhanced through the delegation of responsibilities. When leaders empower employees to take ownership of specific tasks, they increase accountability and motivation. Task ownership fosters a sense of pride and commitment among team members, as they recognize their roles in achieving collective goals. This empowerment aligns with behavior modification techniques that encourage initiative and problem-solving, ultimately leading to increased job satisfaction and lower turnover rates.

Effective behavioral coaching is essential in a task-oriented leadership style, as it enables leaders to cultivate a high-performing team. By providing ongoing support and guidance, leaders can help team members recognize and modify behaviors that may be obstructing their performance. This coaching approach involves regular check-ins, mentoring, and providing resources to develop skills necessary for task completion. When leaders invest in their team's growth through behavior modification and coaching, they not only enhance individual capabilities but also contribute to a culture of continuous improvement, setting the stage for sustained team success.

Balancing Task Orientation with Team Dynamics

Balancing task orientation with team dynamics is a critical challenge for managers and leaders aiming to cultivate high- performing teams. Task orientation emphasizes the importance of clearly defined objectives, structured processes, and measurable outcomes. However, an excessive focus on tasks can inadvertently undermine the interpersonal relationships and collaborative spirit that are essential for a cohesive team environment. To ensure that teams thrive, leaders must find a synergy between accomplishing tasks and fostering a supportive team culture.

One effective approach to achieving this balance is through behavior modification techniques that focus on encouraging positive interactions among team members. By reinforcing collaborative behaviors, such as open communication, mutual respect, and shared problem-solving, leaders can create an environment where task completion does not come at the expense of team cohesion.

Regular feedback sessions can serve as a platform

for recognizing individual contributions while also highlighting the importance of teamwork in achieving broader organizational goals.

Another key aspect of balancing task orientation with team dynamics is the implementation of leadership approaches that prioritize both accountability and empowerment. Leaders should clearly communicate task expectations while simultaneously empowering team members to take ownership of their roles. This dual focus not only increases employee engagement but also enhances motivation, as individuals feel more invested in the outcomes of their contributions. Encouraging team members to set personal goals aligned with team objectives fosters a sense of responsibility and collaboration, driving performance in both areas.

Additionally, behavioral coaching can play a pivotal role in enhancing team performance by addressing both task-related behaviors and team dynamics. Through targeted coaching, leaders can help team members identify and modify behaviors that may hinder collaboration or task execution. Providing tools and strategies for effective communication, conflict resolution, and constructive feedback enables employees to navigate interpersonal challenges while remaining focused on their tasks. This holistic approach to development ensures that individual and team performance metrics align, ultimately enhancing overall productivity.

Finally, evaluating performance metrics through a dual lens of task achievement and team dynamics can provide valuable insights for leaders. Metrics should not solely focus on individual task completion but also incorporate measures of teamwork, collaboration, and employee engagement. By analyzing these metrics, leaders can identify areas for improvement and recognize patterns that may indicate underlying issues within team dynamics. This comprehensive evaluation approach encourages continuous improvement and reinforces the importance of balancing task orientation with a healthy team culture, ultimately leading to sustainable high performance.

Case Studies of Successful Task-Oriented Leaders

In the realm of task-oriented leadership, case studies often illuminate the effective strategies employed by successful leaders who prioritize tasks over individuals. One notable example is the approach taken by a project manager at a technology firm. Faced with a tight deadline for software development, the leader implemented a clear task allocation system that allowed team members to take ownership of specific components of the project. By utilizing performance metrics to track progress, the team maintained a sharp focus on outcomes rather than on interpersonal dynamics. This clarity resulted in a 25% increase in project efficiency and fostered an environment where employees felt empowered to contribute meaningfully, demonstrating the effectiveness of task-oriented leadership.

Another case study can be found in the nonprofit sector, where a director of operations adopted behavior modification techniques to enhance team performance. By identifying key behaviors that hindered productivity, such as procrastination and lack of accountability, the leader introduced structured weekly reviews. These sessions encouraged team members to reflect on their task completion and set actionable goals for the following week. The result was a significant increase in task completion rates, alongside an increase in overall team morale. This leader's focus on behavioral coaching and task ownership not only improved performance metrics but also cultivated a culture of continuous improvement within the organization.

In the manufacturing industry, a plant manager exemplified task-oriented leadership through the implementation of a performance-based reward system. By linking incentives directly to task completion and quality metrics, the manager motivated team members to focus on their specific roles and responsibilities. This strategy not only enhanced productivity but also reduced errors on the production line. The success of this approach highlights the importance of aligning employee engagement with clear task objectives, demonstrating that when team members understand how their contributions impact overall goals, they are more likely to excel in their roles.

A case study from the retail sector illustrates how a store manager utilized behavioral modification techniques to transform team dynamics. By conducting regular training sessions on effective task management and providing real-time feedback, the manager fostered an environment where employees felt accountable for their performance. The store saw a marked improvement in customer satisfaction scores, attributed to the team's increased focus on completing tasks efficiently. This case underscores the significance of continuous behavioral coaching and the impact it can have on team performance and customer engagement.

Lastly, in the financial services industry, a team leader adopted a task-oriented approach to navigate a challenging market. By establishing clear performance metrics and regularly reviewing team progress, the leader ensured that all members remained focused on their individual and collective tasks. This structured approach not only led to improved efficiency but also helped the team adapt quickly to changing market conditions. The leader's commitment to task orientation, coupled with a focus on behavior modification, resulted in enhanced overall team performance, demonstrating that effective leadership in task management can drive significant organizational success.

Chapter 6: Employee Engagement Through Task Ownership

The Importance of Task Ownership

The concept of task ownership is pivotal in fostering a high-performing workplace where employees feel empowered and accountable for their contributions. When team members take ownership of their tasks, they become more engaged and invested in the outcomes of their work. This sense of ownership encourages individuals to go beyond mere compliance, driving them to innovate and seek solutions actively. Managers and leaders must understand that by promoting task ownership, they are not just delegating responsibilities but also cultivating an environment where each team member feels a personal stake in the organization's success.

Effective task ownership is cultivated through clear expectations and structured responsibility. Leaders should clearly define roles and responsibilities, ensuring team members understand what is expected of them. This clarity minimizes confusion and provides a framework for accountability. When employees know their specific tasks and how they contribute to broader organizational goals, they are more likely to take initiative and seek improvements in their work processes.

Leaders can enhance this sense of ownership by involving employees in decision-making processes related to their tasks, allowing them to voice their insights and suggestions.

In addition to clarity, fostering an environment that supports task ownership requires consistent behavioral coaching. Managers should focus on reinforcing positive behaviors associated with task completion and collaboration. By recognizing and rewarding proactive approaches, leaders can motivate their teams to embrace responsibility fully.

Behavioral coaching also involves addressing and correcting misalignments in task execution without pointing fingers at individuals. Instead, the focus should remain on behaviors and processes, promoting a growth mindset that encourages continuous improvement and learning.

Engaging employees through task ownership not only enhances individual performance but also strengthens team dynamics. When employees feel responsible for their tasks, they are more likely to collaborate and communicate effectively with their colleagues. This synergy fosters a culture of mutual support, where team members can share insights, resources, and feedback, ultimately leading to higher quality outcomes. Leaders should actively facilitate this collaboration by creating opportunities for team interactions, such as brainstorming sessions or project debriefs, reinforcing the idea that collective ownership drives success.

To measure the impact of task ownership, organizations should develop performance metrics that focus on task-based assessments. These metrics should evaluate not only the completion of tasks but also the quality and innovation demonstrated in their execution.

By shifting the focus from traditional performance reviews to task-centric evaluations, leaders can better understand individual contributions and identify areas for development. This approach not only reinforces the importance of task ownership but also provides valuable insights for ongoing training and support, ultimately leading to a more engaged and high-performing team.

Strategies to Foster Engagement and Ownership

Creating an environment that fosters engagement and ownership among team members requires a strategic approach that aligns with the principles of behavior modification. Managers and leaders must focus on establishing clear expectations and providing the necessary resources for employees to take ownership of their tasks. This begins with clearly defined roles and responsibilities, ensuring that each team member understands how their contributions align with the organization's goals. By setting specific, measurable performance metrics, leaders can direct attention toward the output and behaviors that drive success, thereby enhancing accountability and ownership.

One effective strategy is to implement a system of behavioral coaching that encourages ongoing feedback and reinforcement. Rather than solely evaluating performance through traditional assessments, leaders should engage in regular one-on-one sessions that emphasize positive behaviors and tactics for improvement. This coaching model empowers employees to reflect on their performance and identify areas for growth. By fostering a culture of open communication, leaders can ensure that employees feel supported and motivated to embrace their roles fully, leading to higher levels of engagement and satisfaction.

In addition to coaching, creating opportunities for team collaboration can significantly enhance ownership. When team members are involved in decision-making processes related to their tasks, they are more likely to feel a sense of ownership and commitment to their work. Leaders should facilitate collaborative environments where employees can share ideas, brainstorm solutions, and collectively address challenges. This not only strengthens team dynamics but also promotes a sense of shared responsibility, as team members become invested in the outcomes of their collaborative efforts.

Recognizing and rewarding task ownership is another vital strategy for fostering engagement. Leaders must implement recognition programs that highlight individual and team accomplishments related to task performance. By celebrating successes, teams are motivated to continue pursuing excellence in their tasks. Recognition should be specific and tied to the behaviors that contribute to high performance, reinforcing the notion that ownership and accountability lead to positive results. This not only enhances morale but also strengthens the connection between individual behaviors and organizational success.

Finally, continuous learning and development opportunities are essential for nurturing engagement and ownership. Managers should encourage employees to pursue professional development that aligns with their roles and interests. This commitment to growth not only enhances individual skills but also empowers employees to take greater ownership of their tasks, as they feel equipped to tackle challenges and innovate within their roles. By prioritizing learning, leaders create a dynamic workplace where employees are engaged, accountable, and motivated to contribute to the team's overall success.

Measuring the Impact of Task Ownership on Performance

Measuring the impact of task ownership on performance is crucial for managers and leaders seeking to optimize their teams. Task ownership refers to the degree to which employees feel responsible for their assigned tasks and outcomes. When employees take ownership of their tasks, they exhibit higher levels of engagement, motivation, and accountability. This sense of ownership can be quantified through various performance metrics, including productivity rates, quality of work, and overall team morale. By understanding these metrics, leaders can assess how effectively task ownership translates into improved performance and identify areas for further enhancement.

One of the primary methods for measuring the impact of task ownership is through performance reviews that focus on specific, task-oriented objectives. Managers can establish clear expectations and benchmarks for each task, ensuring that employees understand their responsibilities. Regular feedback sessions can be conducted to evaluate how well individuals are meeting these objectives, allowing leaders to gauge the correlation between task ownership and various performance indicators. Additionally, utilizing 360-degree feedback can provide a comprehensive view of how task ownership affects team dynamics and overall performance.

Employee engagement surveys are another valuable tool for measuring the impact of task ownership. By regularly assessing employees' feelings of ownership and commitment to their tasks, managers can gather insights into the level of engagement within their teams. These surveys can include questions about employees' perceptions of autonomy, accountability, and the importance of their contributions. Analyzing the results can help leaders identify patterns and make informed decisions about how to foster a culture of ownership, ultimately enhancing team performance.

Another effective approach to measuring task ownership's impact is through project outcomes and success rates. By tracking the completion rates of tasks and projects alongside employee engagement levels, leaders can identify a direct link between ownership and performance. High completion rates and positive project outcomes often correlate with employees who feel a strong sense of ownership over their work. This data can be instrumental in refining task assignment processes and ensuring that individuals are matched with tasks that align with their strengths and interests.

Incorporating behavioral coaching into performance assessments can further illuminate the relationship between task ownership and team performance. Coaches can work with employees to develop a deeper understanding of their roles and the significance of their contributions. By focusing on behavioral modifications that promote ownership, such as setting personal goals and fostering accountability, managers can enhance individual and team performance

.

Ultimately, measuring the impact of task

ownership on performance provides leaders with critical insights that can drive strategic initiatives aimed at building high-performing teams.

Chapter 7: Behavioral Coaching for Enhanced Team Performance

The Role of Coaching in Behavior Modification

Coaching plays a pivotal role in behavior modification, particularly in environments where managers and leaders aim to cultivate high-performing teams. It serves as a structured approach to influence and enhance employee behaviors that directly impact productivity and team dynamics. By focusing on specific behaviors rather than on individual personalities, coaching aligns with the principle that effective management addresses tasks and the behaviors associated with them. This principle is critical in fostering a culture where team members feel supported in their development and are encouraged to take ownership of their tasks.

Behavior modification techniques utilized in coaching empower managers to identify and reinforce positive behaviors while addressing those that hinder performance. This process often involves setting clear expectations and providing continuous feedback, which are essential for guiding team members. Through regular coaching sessions, leaders can teach employees how to adapt their behaviors to meet organizational goals. This not only enhances individual performance but also contributes to the collective success of the team. The focus on behavior rather than individual shortcomings creates an environment where employees feel safe to experiment and grow.

Leadership approaches that emphasize task orientation are particularly effective when paired with behavioral coaching. By framing coaching conversations around specific tasks, leaders can connect desired behaviors to measurable outcomes. This strategic alignment ensures that employees understand the importance of their actions in achieving team objectives. Furthermore, when leaders model task-oriented behaviors themselves, they set a standard that encourages team members to follow suit. This alignment of expectations between leaders and employees fosters a cohesive culture of performance and accountability.

Employee engagement is significantly enhanced through task ownership, a concept that is reinforced by effective coaching. When managers provide guidance that encourages team members to take responsibility for their roles, employees become more invested in their work. Coaching helps establish a sense of autonomy, allowing individuals to recognize the impact of their behaviors on overall team performance. Engaged employees are more likely to exhibit proactive behaviors, seek solutions to challenges, and collaborate effectively with their peers. This heightened engagement ultimately leads to improved productivity and job satisfaction.

Performance metrics for task-based assessments are crucial in evaluating the effectiveness of coaching in behavior modification. By establishing clear, quantifiable goals, managers can track progress and identify areas for further development. Regular assessments allow leaders to tailor their coaching strategies to meet the evolving needs of their teams. This data-driven approach not only validates the impact of behavioral coaching but also reinforces a commitment to continuous improvement. Ultimately, the integration of coaching into behavior modification strategies fosters a high-performing team culture where employees are empowered to excel in their tasks and contribute meaningfully to organizational success.

Techniques for Effective Behavioral Coaching

Effective behavioral coaching is essential for fostering high-performing teams and achieving organizational objectives. Managers and leaders must embrace techniques that emphasize task-oriented management while addressing behaviors that impact performance. One of the foundational techniques is active observation, where leaders closely monitor team dynamics and individual contributions. By paying attention to how tasks are approached and completed, managers can identify specific behaviors that contribute to success or hinder progress. This hands-on approach not only allows for timely interventions but also fosters a culture of accountability, as team members become aware that their actions are being observed and valued.

Another vital technique is the use of constructive feedback. Providing regular, specific feedback helps employees understand the connection between their behaviors and performance outcomes.

Leaders should focus on both positive reinforcement and corrective guidance, ensuring that feedback is framed in a way that emphasizes improvement rather than criticism. This approach encourages team members to take ownership of their tasks and behaviors, as they recognize the direct impact they have on team performance. When feedback is delivered in a timely manner, it reinforces desired behaviors and motivates individuals to adapt and grow.

Goal-setting is a powerful technique in behavioral coaching that aligns individual objectives with team goals. By setting clear, measurable, and achievable performance metrics, managers can guide employees towards specific behavioral changes that enhance task performance. Utilizing the SMART criteria—Specific, Measurable, Achievable, Relevant, and Time-bound— ensures that goals are well-defined and actionable. This not only aids in tracking progress but also instills a sense of purpose and direction among team members, fostering engagement and commitment to their roles.

Incorporating role-playing and scenario-based training is another effective technique for behavioral coaching. This interactive method allows team members to practice their responses to various workplace situations in a controlled environment. By simulating real-life challenges, employees can develop problem- solving skills and learn to adjust their behaviors in response to different scenarios.

Role-playing fosters collaboration and communication among team members, enhancing their ability to work together effectively. Furthermore, it provides an opportunity for leaders to observe behavior in action and offer targeted coaching based on the outcomes of these exercises.

Finally, promoting a culture of continuous improvement through regular check-ins and progress assessments is crucial for effective behavioral coaching. Managers should schedule routine meetings to discuss achievements, challenges, and areas for growth. These discussions should focus on behavior modifications that align with task completion and overall team performance. By creating an open dialogue, leaders can encourage employees to share their perspectives and experiences, fostering a collaborative environment where everyone feels valued and empowered to contribute.

Ultimately, these techniques not only enhance individual performance but also drive the collective success of the team, reinforcing the importance of behavior modification in achieving high performance in the workplace.

Setting Coaching Goals for Team Performance

Setting coaching goals for team performance involves a strategic approach that aligns with the overall objectives of the organization while focusing on individual behaviors that contribute to group success. Managers and leaders must first identify the specific performance metrics relevant to their teams. These metrics not only help in evaluating current performance but also serve as benchmarks for setting realistic and attainable coaching goals. By concentrating on measurable outcomes, leaders can foster a culture of accountability and motivation, ensuring that each team member understands their contribution to the team's success.

To effectively establish coaching goals, it is essential to engage team members in the goal-setting process. This collaborative approach enhances employee engagement and promotes ownership of tasks. When team members are involved in defining their own goals, they are more likely to feel invested in the outcomes. Managers should facilitate discussions that allow team members to express their aspirations and potential challenges. This practice not only strengthens interpersonal relationships but also leads to a clearer understanding of individual roles within the team dynamic.

Behavior modification techniques play a crucial role in reinforcing desired behaviors that align with the established coaching goals. Managers should utilize positive reinforcement strategies to encourage team members when they exhibit behaviors that contribute to achieving team objectives. This could involve recognizing individual contributions publicly or providing incentives for reaching specific milestones. By maintaining a focus on behavior rather than the individual, leaders can create an environment where team members feel supported in their development and motivated to improve continuously.

Another vital aspect of setting coaching goals is to ensure they are aligned with the organization's mission and values. This alignment helps to create a cohesive team that is focused on common objectives.

Leaders should regularly communicate how individual and team goals contribute to broader organizational goals, fostering a sense of purpose among team members. When employees understand how their tasks fit into the larger picture, they are more likely to remain engaged and committed to their roles, resulting in enhanced team performance.

Lastly, regular assessment and feedback are essential components of the coaching process. Managers must establish a routine for evaluating progress towards the set goals and providing constructive feedback. This ongoing dialogue helps to identify areas for improvement and reinforces positive behaviors. By creating a culture of continuous feedback, leaders can ensure that coaching goals evolve alongside team dynamics and organizational needs, ultimately driving sustained high performance.

Chapter 8: Performance Metrics for Task-Based Assessments

Identifying Key Performance Indicators

Identifying key performance indicators (KPIs) is a crucial step in establishing a framework for evaluating team performance within a task-oriented leadership approach. KPIs serve as quantifiable measures that reflect the critical success factors of an organization, enabling managers and leaders to monitor progress and make informed decisions. In the context of behavior modification, KPIs should align with specific behaviors that contribute to desired outcomes, rather than focusing solely on individual performance. This shift in perspective allows leaders to create an environment where tasks are prioritized, and behaviors are nurtured for optimal team efficiency.

To effectively identify KPIs, managers must first define the core objectives of their teams. This involves a thorough analysis of organizational goals, team dynamics, and the specific tasks that drive success. Once these objectives are clear, leaders can develop KPIs that are directly linked to the behaviors that lead to task completion. For instance, if a team's goal is to enhance project delivery times, relevant KPIs might include the average time taken to complete specific tasks and the frequency of task completion within deadlines. These indicators not only provide insight into performance but also highlight areas where behavioral modifications may be necessary.

It is also essential for managers to engage their teams in the process of identifying KPIs. Involving employees in this dialogue fosters a sense of ownership and accountability, which is vital for enhancing employee engagement. When team members understand how their behaviors contribute to the achievement of KPIs, they are more likely to take proactive steps to align their actions with organizational goals. This collaborative approach can also lead to the discovery of additional behavioral metrics that may have otherwise been overlooked, enriching the overall performance assessment framework.

After establishing KPIs, regular monitoring and evaluation are necessary to ensure they remain relevant and effective. Managers should implement a system for tracking these indicators consistently, providing feedback to team members on their progress. This feedback loop is essential for behavioral coaching, as it allows leaders to identify patterns and make necessary adjustments in real-time. By focusing on behavior modification in response to KPI data, leaders can guide their teams toward improved performance while reinforcing the importance of task ownership.

Finally, it is crucial to communicate the significance of KPIs to the entire team. Leaders should articulate how these indicators connect to broader organizational objectives and the role each team member plays in achieving them. This transparency not only motivates employees but also reinforces the idea that performance metrics are tools for growth rather than punitive measures. By fostering an environment where KPIs are viewed as a means for continuous improvement, managers can cultivate high- performing teams that thrive on task-oriented collaboration and behavior modification.

Designing Task-Based Assessment Tools

Designing task-based assessment tools is a crucial component in managing high-performing teams. These tools serve as structured methods to evaluate both individual and team performance, focusing on the completion of specific tasks rather than the people carrying them out. By centering assessments on the tasks themselves, leaders can create a clear framework that aligns employee engagement with organizational goals. This approach minimizes subjectivity and promotes accountability, ensuring that evaluations are based on measurable outcomes rather than personal biases or relationships.

A well-designed task-based assessment tool should encompass clear performance metrics that are directly tied to the organization's objectives. These metrics should be specific, measurable, achievable, relevant, and time- bound (SMART), providing a robust foundation for evaluating performance. For instance, if a team is responsible for a marketing campaign, metrics might include the number of leads generated or the conversion rate of those leads. By focusing on quantifiable outcomes, managers can foster a culture of transparency and continuous improvement, where team members are motivated to take ownership of their tasks and understand their impact on the broader organizational goals.

In developing these assessment tools, behavioral coaching plays a significant role in enhancing team performance. Leaders should integrate feedback mechanisms within the assessment process that empower employees to reflect on their behaviors and outcomes.

This approach not only helps in identifying areas for improvement but also reinforces positive behaviors that contribute to task success. By providing constructive feedback and focusing on specific behaviors linked to task completion, managers can guide their teams towards higher performance levels while simultaneously promoting a culture of learning and development.

Engagement is another critical aspect of task-based assessments. When employees feel that their contributions to tasks are recognized and valued, their intrinsic motivation increases, leading to greater job satisfaction and performance. Leaders should design assessment tools that allow for self-assessment and peer evaluations, encouraging team members to take ownership of their tasks and hold each other accountable. This fosters a sense of community and collaboration within teams, as employees are not only responsible for their own performance but also for supporting their colleagues in achieving shared objectives.

Finally, ongoing evaluation and refinement of task-based assessment tools are essential to adapt to changing organizational needs and team dynamics. Managers should regularly review the effectiveness of their assessment metrics, soliciting input from team members to ensure that the tools remain relevant and impactful. Through iterative feedback and continuous improvement, leaders can cultivate an environment that not only values performance but also prioritizes the development of skills and behaviors that drive success. This proactive approach ensures that task-based assessments remain aligned with the evolving goals of the organization, ultimately leading to sustained high performance and engagement among teams.

Analyzing Performance Data for Continuous Improvement

Analyzing performance data is a crucial aspect of fostering continuous improvement within high-performing teams. For managers and leaders, understanding how to effectively interpret and utilize performance metrics can significantly enhance task-oriented management approaches. This analysis is not merely about reviewing numbers; it involves a deep dive into the behaviors that drive those metrics. By focusing on behavioral outcomes rather than individual performance, leaders can create an environment that prioritizes growth, engagement, and accountability.

To begin with, it is essential to identify the right performance metrics that align with organizational goals and team objectives. Metrics should be carefully selected to reflect the tasks that teams are responsible for, rather than focusing solely on individual achievements. This task-oriented approach encourages collaboration and shared accountability among team members.

Managers should prioritize metrics that measure not just results but also the processes and behaviors that lead to those results. This ensures that performance data provides a comprehensive view of team dynamics and effectiveness.

Once performance metrics are in place, the next step is to analyze the data for patterns and insights. This involves looking beyond surface-level results to identify underlying behavioral trends. For instance, if a team consistently meets its targets but struggles with quality, it may indicate a need to address specific behaviors or processes that impact performance. By using data to highlight these behavioral patterns, leaders can implement targeted interventions that modify specific behaviors, ultimately driving better performance outcomes.

Engaging employees in the analysis of performance data can further enhance the effectiveness of this process. When team members are involved in assessing their own performance metrics, they develop a sense of ownership over their tasks and responsibilities. This engagement fosters a culture of accountability where employees are more invested in their individual and collective success. By providing training on how to interpret and utilize performance data, managers can empower their teams to take an active role in their own continuous improvement.

Finally, it's crucial for leaders to establish a feedback loop where insights gained from performance data analysis lead to actionable changes. Regularly scheduled reviews of performance metrics should be integrated into team meetings, allowing for ongoing discussions about progress and areas for improvement. This iterative process not only reinforces the importance of data-driven decision-making but also cultivates an environment where behavioral coaching is embraced. By consistently reinforcing desired behaviors and addressing areas of concern through constructive feedback, leaders can drive sustained improvement and elevate team performance over time.

Chapter 9: Creating a Sustainable Culture of High Performance

Embedding Purpose into Team Culture

Embedding purpose into team culture requires a deliberate focus on aligning individual and collective goals with the overarching mission of the organization. Managers and leaders play a crucial role in facilitating this alignment by clearly communicating the purpose behind team tasks and responsibilities. This connection between purpose and tasks not only enhances clarity but also fosters a sense of belonging among team members. When employees understand how their contributions advance the organization's goals, they are more likely to engage with their work and take ownership of their tasks, resulting in improved performance and morale.

To effectively embed purpose into team culture, leaders must model the behaviors they wish to see in their teams. By demonstrating a strong commitment to the organization's mission and values, leaders can inspire team members to adopt a similar mindset. This involves consistently reinforcing the purpose behind tasks during team meetings, performance reviews, and informal interactions. By integrating purpose into everyday conversations and decision-making processes, managers can create an environment where employees feel valued and motivated to contribute their best efforts.

Behavior modification techniques can be instrumental in reinforcing a purpose-driven culture. By recognizing and rewarding behaviors that align with the team's objectives, leaders can encourage a culture of accountability and ownership. This might involve implementing performance metrics that not only assess task completion but also evaluate how well team members embody the organization's purpose in their work. Such metrics can serve as a powerful motivator, guiding employees to take pride in their contributions while also fostering a deeper connection to the team's mission.

Employee engagement is significantly enhanced

when team members feel a sense of ownership over their tasks. Leaders should empower employees by involving them in goal-setting processes and decision-making, allowing them to see the direct impact of their work on the organization's success. This approach not only encourages accountability but also cultivates a culture where individuals are motivated to perform at their best. By fostering an environment that emphasizes ownership, managers can create a team culture where purpose is not just an abstract concept but an integral part of daily operations.

Finally, the role of behavioral coaching cannot be understated in embedding purpose into team culture. Leaders who invest time in coaching their team members can help them understand their unique contributions to the organization's mission. This personalized approach not only enhances individual performance but also strengthens team dynamics. By focusing on behavioral improvement and aligning personal goals with team objectives, managers can ensure that purpose permeates the team culture, resulting in high-performing teams that are engaged, motivated, and aligned with the organization's vision.

Strategies for Sustaining High Performance

Sustaining high performance in teams requires a strategic approach that prioritizes task management over traditional people management. By focusing on the tasks themselves, managers can create a culture where employees understand their responsibilities and feel empowered to take ownership of their roles. This shift in perspective allows leaders to implement behavior modification techniques that enhance performance by aligning individual behaviors with team goals. By fostering an environment where tasks are the central focus, leaders can encourage accountability and commitment, ultimately driving higher performance levels.

One effective strategy for sustaining high performance is to establish clear performance metrics that align with task-based assessments. These metrics should be specific, measurable, and attainable, providing employees with concrete benchmarks to aim for. By regularly reviewing these metrics, managers can provide timely feedback, reinforcing positive behaviors while addressing areas needing improvement. This continuous cycle of assessment and feedback ensures that employees remain engaged and aware of their contributions to the team's success, fostering a sense of ownership and pride in their work.

Behavioral coaching plays a crucial role in enhancing team performance. Leaders should actively engage with their team members to identify individual strengths and areas for growth. Through targeted coaching sessions, managers can help employees develop the skills necessary to excel in their tasks. This personalized approach not only improves individual performance but also cultivates a collaborative team environment. By investing in the development of their employees, leaders signal their commitment to sustaining high performance and create a culture of continuous improvement.

Employee engagement is further enhanced when organizations create opportunities for task ownership. By involving team members in decision-making processes related to their specific tasks, leaders can increase motivation and accountability. When employees feel that they have a stake in their work, they are more likely to invest their time and energy into achieving high performance. Encouraging autonomy in task management not only boosts morale but also fosters innovation, as employees are more likely to pursue creative solutions and improvements when they feel empowered.

Finally, adopting leadership approaches focused on task orientation is essential for sustaining high performance over the long term. Leaders should model behaviors that prioritize task completion and efficiency, setting an example for their teams. By emphasizing the importance of tasks and the behaviors that lead to successful outcomes, managers can cultivate a culture where high performance is the norm. This approach not only enhances team dynamics but also aligns individual and organizational goals, driving sustained success and resilience in the face of challenges.

Future Trends in Team Leadership and Behavior Modification

The landscape of team leadership is evolving rapidly, necessitating a shift toward a more nuanced understanding of behavior modification within high-performing teams. As managers and leaders, it is crucial to recognize that the future of leadership will increasingly focus on managing tasks rather than individuals. This shift underscores the importance of behavioral approaches that discipline actions and practices rather than the people themselves. By embracing this philosophy, leaders can foster an environment where accountability and ownership are promoted, ultimately enhancing team performance.

Behavior modification techniques are becoming integral to workplace dynamics, allowing leaders to implement structured approaches that influence and enhance employee behavior. These techniques, grounded in psychological principles, encourage positive behavior changes through reinforcement strategies. Future trends indicate that leaders will increasingly rely on data-driven methods to monitor behaviors, providing real-time feedback that can adjust team dynamics effectively. This evolution not only improves individual accountability but also aligns team efforts with organizational goals, enhancing overall productivity.

Task orientation is predicted to be a significant trend in leadership approaches, emphasizing the importance of clear, measurable objectives. By focusing on the tasks at hand, leaders can delineate responsibilities and expectations more effectively. This clarity reduces ambiguity and empowers team members to take ownership of their roles, fostering a sense of responsibility and commitment. As teams become more engaged in their tasks, the overall morale and performance levels are likely to improve, leading to sustained success within the organization.

Employee engagement through task ownership will be a cornerstone of future leadership strategies. By providing team members with autonomy over their assignments, leaders can cultivate a sense of pride and investment in their work. This approach not only enhances motivation but also encourages innovation and creativity among team members. As teams feel more empowered, they are likely to take greater initiative, leading to higher levels of collaboration and problem-solving skills, which are essential in fast-paced work environments.

Behavioral coaching will emerge as a vital tool for enhancing team performance. This coaching model focuses on developing individuals' skills to align their behaviors with team objectives. Leaders will increasingly adopt coaching techniques that facilitate constructive feedback, helping team members identify areas for improvement while celebrating their successes. As performance metrics become more sophisticated and oriented toward task-based assessments, leaders will be better equipped to guide their teams in achieving both personal and organizational goals. This future trend emphasizes the need for continuous learning and adaptation in leadership practices, ultimately driving high performance in teams.

Chapter 10: Conclusion: Leading with Purpose

Recap of Key Concepts

In the realm of effective management, a fundamental principle emerges: we manage tasks, not people. This concept shifts the focus from individual personalities and grievances to the specific responsibilities and projects that drive team success. By emphasizing task management, leaders can create an environment where employees feel accountable for their contributions, fostering a culture of ownership and responsibility. This approach not only clarifies expectations but also allows for a more objective evaluation of performance, enabling managers to align team efforts with organizational goals.

Disciplining behaviors, not people, is another crucial concept that underpins effective leadership. By concentrating on the behaviors that lead to desired outcomes, managers can implement corrective measures without placing blame on individuals. This behavior modification technique encourages a constructive feedback loop, where employees are guided to understand the impact of their actions on team performance. By focusing on behaviors, leaders can cultivate an atmosphere where improvement is achievable and progress is celebrated, leading to higher morale and motivation among team members.

Behavior modification techniques play a pivotal role in enhancing workplace dynamics. These techniques encompass a range of strategies aimed at reinforcing positive behaviors while diminishing negative ones.

Managers can utilize methods such as reinforcement, modeling, and feedback to shape desired behaviors. For instance, recognizing and rewarding employees for collaborative efforts not only reinforces teamwork but also encourages others to adopt similar practices. By systematically applying these techniques, leaders can create a high-performing team that thrives on shared objectives rather than individual competition.

Task-oriented leadership approaches further

complement the goal of employee engagement through task ownership. When leaders adopt a task-oriented mindset, they clearly define roles and responsibilities, allowing team members to take ownership of their work. This sense of ownership is crucial for fostering engagement, as employees feel empowered to make decisions and contribute meaningfully to projects. Task ownership leads to increased accountability, as individuals recognize that their performance directly influences team outcomes. In this environment, team members are more likely to take initiative, leading to enhanced overall performance.

Finally, performance metrics for task-based assessments provide a concrete means of evaluating individual and team contributions. By establishing clear, measurable outcomes aligned with organizational objectives, managers can assess performance in a fair and transparent manner. These metrics not only serve as a benchmark for success but also guide ongoing development efforts. As teams work towards these metrics, they gain insights into their strengths and areas for improvement, fostering a continuous growth mindset. By emphasizing task-based assessments, leaders can ensure that their teams remain focused on achieving results that matter, ultimately driving the organization towards its strategic goals.

The Future of Purpose-Driven Leadership

The future of purpose-driven leadership is poised to redefine how managers and leaders approach their roles in organizations. As the workplace continues to evolve with technological advancements and shifting employee expectations, leaders must adapt their strategies to foster a culture of engagement and accountability. Purpose-driven leadership emphasizes the importance of aligning team members' individual goals with the overarching mission of the organization. This alignment not only enhances employee motivation but also drives a sense of belonging, which is crucial in high- performing teams.

In an era where tasks take precedence over traditional people management, leaders will increasingly adopt behavior modification techniques that focus on reinforcing positive actions rather than merely correcting negative ones. This shift will require leaders to develop a keen understanding of behavioral psychology and its applications in the workplace. By employing techniques such as positive reinforcement and constructive feedback, leaders can create an environment where employees feel valued and empowered to take ownership of their tasks. This approach not only improves individual performance but also cultivates a collaborative team dynamic.

Task-oriented leadership approaches will become more prevalent as organizations recognize the significance of clear objectives and measurable outcomes. Leaders will need to set specific performance metrics that align with both team and organizational goals. By fostering a results-driven culture, leaders will encourage employees to take initiative and demonstrate ownership over their work. This focus on tasks will allow for more effective assessments and evaluations, ensuring that everyone understands their contributions to the team's success.

Employee engagement will be significantly enhanced through the implementation of behavioral coaching strategies. Managers who prioritize coaching over traditional supervision will empower their teams to develop skills and confidence in their abilities. This shift in focus will allow leaders to become facilitators of growth rather than mere overseers of tasks. By providing ongoing support and constructive feedback, leaders can help team members identify areas for improvement and celebrate their achievements, thereby creating an atmosphere of continuous development.

As the landscape of work continues to evolve, purpose-driven leadership will require a commitment to lifelong learning and adaptability. Leaders must stay attuned to emerging trends and be willing to embrace innovative practices that promote task ownership and behavioral change. By fostering a culture that values purpose, accountability, and engagement, leaders can ensure their teams remain resilient and high-performing in the face of challenges. The future of leadership lies in understanding that effective management is not just about overseeing work but inspiring individuals to connect their personal aspirations with the collective goals of the organization.

Call to Action for Managers and Leaders

In today's fast-paced work environment, managers and leaders must embrace a paradigm shift that focuses on managing tasks rather than people. This approach not only enhances efficiency but also fosters an atmosphere where employees feel empowered and engaged. By concentrating on the specific tasks at hand, leaders can delineate clear objectives and expectations that guide team members in their roles. This clarity allows for a structured work environment where accountability is a shared responsibility between managers and team members, ultimately leading to higher performance and satisfaction.

Disciplining behaviors, rather than individuals, is a cornerstone of effective leadership in task-oriented environments. It is essential for managers to recognize that behaviors can be modified through constructive feedback and reinforcement. By setting behavioral standards tied to specific tasks, leaders can create a culture of accountability without personalizing performance issues. This not only promotes a healthier workplace dynamic but also encourages employees to take ownership of their actions, leading to improved morale and productivity. When behaviors are addressed with the intent to improve rather than punish, teams can adapt and evolve more effectively.

Implementing behavior modification techniques in the workplace is crucial for enhancing team performance. Managers should utilize strategies such as positive reinforcement, goal setting, and regular performance reviews that focus on task completion and behavior alignment. By providing consistent feedback and recognizing achievements, leaders can motivate employees to engage more deeply with their tasks. This proactive approach to behavior modification fosters a growth mindset, where team members view challenges as opportunities for development rather than obstacles.

Leadership approaches that prioritize task orientation are vital in cultivating employee engagement through task ownership.

Managers should encourage autonomy by allowing team members to take the lead on projects, which instills a sense of responsibility and pride in their work. When employees feel that they have a stake in the outcome of their tasks, they are more likely to be invested in their performance. This empowerment is essential for creating a high-performing team where individuals are motivated to contribute their best efforts.

Lastly, establishing performance metrics for task-based assessments is essential for measuring and guiding team success.

Managers should develop clear, quantifiable benchmarks that align with organizational goals and objectives. By regularly reviewing these metrics, leaders can identify areas for improvement and celebrate achievements, creating a continuous feedback loop that drives performance. This data-driven approach not only informs decision-making but also reinforces the importance of task-oriented behaviors, ensuring that teams remain focused on achieving their goals while fostering a culture of excellence.

Chapter 11: Quick Decision-Making Frameworks

The Importance of Swift Decisions

The ability to make swift decisions is a critical skill for managers and business leaders navigating the fast-paced corporate environment. In today's world, where information is abundant and the margin for error is slim, the capacity to evaluate options quickly and act decisively can significantly impact both individual and organizational success. Swift decision-making not only enhances productivity but also fosters a culture of agility within teams, allowing organizations to adapt to changes more effectively and seize opportunities as they arise.

Implementing quick decision-making frameworks can streamline processes and improve efficiency. Techniques such as the Eisenhower Matrix or the OODA Loop encourage managers to categorize tasks based on urgency and importance or to observe, orient, decide, and act, respectively. These frameworks enable leaders to prioritize effectively and make informed choices under pressure. By adopting such methodologies, managers can reduce indecision and enhance their team's responsiveness, ensuring that critical decisions are made in a timely manner.

Moreover, swift decisions often lead to faster conflict resolution. When conflicts arise, a prompt response can prevent issues from escalating and maintain team cohesion.

Utilizing instant conflict resolution tactics, such as active listening and seeking common ground, allows managers to address disputes quickly and constructively. This not only restores harmony but also reinforces a culture of open communication, where team members feel valued and are more likely to engage positively in future discussions.

In addition to resolving conflicts, quick decision-making plays a vital role in goal setting and prioritization. Effective managers recognize that clarity and direction are essential for their teams. By establishing rapid goal-setting techniques, such as the SMART criteria, leaders can ensure that objectives are specific, measurable, achievable, relevant, and time-bound. This clarity allows teams to focus their efforts on what truly matters, aligning their actions with the organization's strategic vision while adapting to changes as they occur.

Finally, the importance of swift decisions extends to performance feedback and change management. Regular, efficient feedback sessions can guide employees toward improvement and development, while embracing change requires prompt decision-making to adapt strategies and processes.

Simple approaches, like one-minute coaching techniques, empower managers to provide immediate, constructive feedback that drives performance. By fostering an environment where swift decisions are encouraged, leaders can cultivate a proactive organizational culture that thrives on innovation and resilience.

The 4D Decision Model

The 4D Decision Model is a framework designed to streamline decision-making processes for busy managers and business leaders. It emphasizes four key dimensions: Define, Develop, Decide, and Deliver. By using this model, managers can cut through the noise of complex decisions and focus on actionable steps that lead to effective outcomes. The 4D Decision Model is particularly useful in fast-paced environments where time is of the essence, allowing leaders to make informed choices quickly.

In the Define phase, managers clarify the problem at hand and gather relevant information. This involves identifying the core issue, understanding the context, and setting clear objectives. Busy managers often face multiple challenges simultaneously, so taking a moment to articulate the decision's purpose helps in aligning team efforts. A well-defined problem not only guides the decision-making process but also ensures that all stakeholders share a common understanding, reducing potential conflicts later on.

Moving to the Develop phase, leaders explore potential solutions. This stage encourages creativity and collaboration, inviting team members to contribute ideas. Managers should leverage brainstorming sessions or digital tools to generate a variety of options. By fostering an inclusive environment where team input is valued, managers can uncover innovative solutions that may not have surfaced through individual contemplation.

This phase is critical for ensuring that all possible avenues are explored before narrowing down choices.

Once a range of solutions has been developed, the next step is the Decide phase. Here, managers must evaluate the options against the defined objectives and criteria established in the previous phases. This evaluation process can be expedited by using decision-making tools such as pros and cons lists or prioritization matrices. By applying these techniques, managers can quickly assess which options offer the best potential for success and align with the organization's goals. This phase is pivotal, as it transforms ideas into actionable plans.

Finally, the Deliver phase focuses on executing the chosen solution and monitoring its impact. Successful implementation requires clear communication of the decision to all relevant parties and outlining specific action steps. Managers should establish metrics for success and regularly review progress to ensure that the decision leads to the desired outcomes. By following the 4D Decision Model, leaders not only enhance their decision-making efficiency but also foster a culture of accountability and continuous improvement within their teams.

Utilizing the Eisenhower Matrix

Utilizing the Eisenhower Matrix is a powerful tool for managers and business leaders seeking to enhance their decision-making and prioritization skills. This framework, also known as the Urgent-Important Matrix, categorizes tasks into four quadrants based on their urgency and importance. By distinguishing between what is urgent and what truly matters, leaders can allocate their time and resources more effectively, ensuring that they focus on activities that drive significant results rather than merely responding to immediate pressures.

The first quadrant contains tasks that are both urgent and important. These are the crises and deadlines that demand immediate attention and often require swift action.

Managers should prioritize these tasks, ensuring they are addressed promptly to prevent larger issues from arising. However, it's essential to recognize that continually operating in this quadrant can lead to burnout and a reactive management style. Leaders should aim to minimize the number of tasks in this category by anticipating challenges and planning accordingly.

The second quadrant focuses on tasks that are important but not urgent. This area is where strategic planning, relationship building, and personal development reside. By dedicating time to these activities, managers can proactively shape their work environment and develop their teams. Allocating resources to this quadrant fosters innovation and prevents the crises that typically arise from neglecting important tasks. It is a space for setting long-term goals and ensuring that the team is aligned with the organization's vision.

The third quadrant includes tasks that are urgent but not important. These often involve interruptions or demands from others that can distract leaders from their core responsibilities. It is crucial for managers to learn how to delegate or defer these tasks where possible.

By empowering team members to handle these urgent but less critical tasks, leaders can reclaim valuable time for more significant initiatives, thus enhancing overall productivity and focus.

Finally, the fourth quadrant consists of tasks that are neither urgent nor important. These activities can lead to wasted time and should be minimized or eliminated altogether.

Managers should regularly assess their schedules and identify any time-wasting habits or distractions. By consciously reducing the time spent in this quadrant, leaders can create more space for important work, ultimately leading to better outcomes for themselves and their teams. By consistently applying the Eisenhower Matrix, managers can cultivate a more efficient and effective approach to their leadership responsibilities.

The 5-Second Rule for Timely Choices

The 5-Second Rule for Timely Choices is a powerful technique that can significantly enhance decision-making for managers and business leaders. This rule is based on the premise that when faced with a choice, individuals should count down from five and then commit to a decision. The countdown creates a sense of urgency that can help bypass overthinking and second-guessing, which often lead to indecision and missed opportunities. By adhering to this simple framework, managers can foster a culture of swift decision-making within their teams, enabling a more agile and responsive work environment.

Implementing the 5-Second Rule requires practice and discipline. When confronted with a decision, take a moment to assess the options, then initiate the countdown. This approach not only encourages personal accountability but also instills confidence in team members. Managers can model this behavior by making timely decisions in meetings, demonstrating that hesitation can hinder progress. The key is to recognize that not every decision needs to be perfect; rather, taking action is often more beneficial than remaining paralyzed by analysis.

Furthermore, the 5-Second Rule can be particularly effective in high-pressure situations where fast decisions are crucial. For example, when a conflict arises within a team, leaders can apply this technique to swiftly determine the next steps instead of allowing the situation to escalate. By acting quickly, managers can diffuse tension and redirect focus toward constructive solutions. This swift response not only resolves issues but also reinforces the importance of timely action in maintaining team cohesion and morale.

Incorporating the 5-Second Rule into regular team

practices can also enhance goal-setting and prioritization efforts. During planning sessions, managers can encourage team members to use this method when deciding on project priorities or resource allocation. By limiting the time spent on deliberation, teams can more effectively align their efforts with organizational objectives. This approach fosters a proactive mindset, where team members feel empowered to make decisions that drive progress without waiting for extensive consultations.

Ultimately, the 5-Second Rule is an invaluable tool for managers seeking to improve their decision-making capabilities. By promoting a culture of rapid choices, leaders can enhance their teams' adaptability and responsiveness in an ever-changing business landscape.

Embracing this technique not only streamlines operations but also cultivates a dynamic work environment where employees feel equipped to tackle challenges head-on. As managers adopt this practice, they will likely see a marked improvement in both individual and team performance, leading to greater organizational success.

Chapter 12: Instant Conflict Resolution Tactics

Understanding Conflict Dynamics

Understanding conflict dynamics is essential for managers and business leaders who aim to maintain a productive work environment.

Conflicts in the workplace are inevitable; they can arise from differing opinions, competition for resources, or varying personal styles.

Understanding these dynamics allows leaders to navigate conflicts more effectively, minimizing disruption and fostering a culture of collaboration. Recognizing the root causes of conflict is the first step in managing it

Leaders must assess whether conflicts stem from miscommunication, differing values, or external pressures, which can inform their approach to resolution.

Effective conflict resolution begins with active listening. Managers should encourage open dialogue among team members, allowing them to express their perspectives without fear of reprisal. This approach not only helps in understanding the underlying issues but also promotes a sense of respect among team members. By creating a safe space for discussion, leaders can facilitate a more constructive exchange of ideas, which can lead to innovative solutions. This technique not only resolves the immediate conflict but also strengthens team cohesion in the long term.

Another critical aspect of understanding conflict dynamics is recognizing the various styles of conflict management. Each individual may approach conflict differently—some may be confrontational, while others may avoid conflict altogether. Leaders should identify these styles within their teams and adapt their strategies accordingly. For instance, using a collaborative approach can lead to win-win outcomes when both parties are willing to engage and find common ground. Conversely, in situations where quick resolution is necessary, a more directive approach may be appropriate to expedite decision-making.

Once a conflict has been addressed, it is vital for leaders to follow up and assess the outcomes of the resolution process. This reflection helps in understanding what worked and what could be improved for future conflicts. Managers can gather feedback from involved parties to evaluate the effectiveness of the resolution and adjust their conflict management strategies accordingly. This not only helps in personal growth as a leader but also reinforces the importance of continuous improvement within the team.

Lastly, fostering a culture of conflict resolution within an organization is crucial. Managers should model positive conflict resolution behaviors and provide training on effective communication and negotiation techniques. By equipping employees with the tools to resolve conflicts independently, leaders create a more resilient workforce. This proactive approach can lead to a significant reduction in workplace tensions and an increase in overall productivity, enabling the organization to thrive even in challenging situations.

The DESC Model for Effective Communication

The DESC model stands for Describe, Express, Specify, and Consequence, and serves as a powerful framework for effective communication, particularly in managerial contexts. This model is designed to facilitate clear and constructive conversations, especially when addressing conflicts or performance issues. By employing the DESC model, managers can ensure that their messages are delivered with clarity and purpose, enabling their teams to understand expectations and the rationale behind decisions.

In the first step of the DESC model, "Describe," managers should focus on objectively stating the situation at hand. This means avoiding personal judgments or emotions and instead providing a factual account of the behavior or issue that needs to be addressed. For instance, rather than saying, "You never meet deadlines," a manager could state, "In the last three projects, the deadlines were missed by an average of two days." This lays a neutral foundation for the conversation and helps prevent defensiveness from the recipient.

The second step, "Express," allows the manager to communicate their feelings about the situation. This is where the emotional impact of the behavior can be conveyed, helping the other party understand the significance of the issue. For example, a manager might say, "I feel concerned when deadlines are missed because it affects our team's overall productivity and client satisfaction." This personal expression fosters empathy and encourages a more open dialogue about the implications of the behavior.

Next, the "Specify" step involves outlining what is expected moving forward. This is crucial for effective communication, as it eliminates ambiguity and provides clear guidelines for improvement. A manager could say, "I would like you to complete your tasks two days before the deadline in future projects." By setting specific expectations, managers can empower their team members to take ownership of their responsibilities and work towards collective goals.

Finally, the "Consequence" step emphasizes the

potential outcomes of adhering to or neglecting the specified expectations. This can include both positive reinforcement and the consequences of continued issues. For instance, a manager might state, "By meeting deadlines, we can enhance our team's reputation and secure more projects. If deadlines are missed consistently, it could lead to decreased client trust." This conclusion reinforces accountability and motivates team members to align their actions with organizational objectives, ultimately contributing to a more effective work environment.

Quick Mediation Techniques

Quick mediation techniques are essential tools for managers and business leaders who need to resolve conflicts swiftly and effectively. In a fast-paced business environment, prolonged disputes can hinder productivity and affect team morale. The following techniques can be implemented in a matter of minutes, allowing leaders to address issues before they escalate and maintain a harmonious workplace.

One effective approach is to use active listening during mediation. This involves giving full attention to the parties involved, acknowledging their feelings, and paraphrasing their concerns to demonstrate understanding. By ensuring that everyone feels heard, managers can create a safe space for open dialogue. This technique not only helps clarify the issues at hand but also fosters an atmosphere of respect, encouraging collaborative problem-solving.

Another quick technique is to establish common ground. Managers can facilitate discussions by identifying shared goals or interests between conflicting parties. By focusing on what both sides want to achieve, leaders can shift the conversation from confrontation to cooperation. This strategy not only expedites the mediation process but also helps build relationships and trust among team members, which is crucial for long-term collaboration.

Additionally, utilizing the "interest-based negotiation" approach can be highly effective.

Instead of concentrating solely on positions or demands, managers should encourage parties to articulate their underlying interests. This technique allows for creative solutions that satisfy the needs of both sides, rather than forcing a compromise that leaves one party dissatisfied. By reframing the conversation around interests, leaders can facilitate quicker resolutions that are more likely to be embraced by all involved.

Finally, setting a clear time limit for discussions can enhance focus and efficiency during mediation. By establishing a specific timeframe, managers encourage participants to express their views concisely and prioritize the most critical issues. This urgency can lead to more decisive outcomes, as parties are motivated to reach a resolution swiftly. It is essential that managers communicate this time constraint positively, emphasizing the goal of arriving at a satisfactory conclusion rather than rushing through the process.

Incorporating these quick mediation techniques into daily management practices enables leaders to address conflicts promptly and effectively. By employing active listening, establishing common ground, focusing on interests, and setting time limits, managers can foster a productive work environment where conflicts are resolved efficiently. These skills not only enhance interpersonal relationships but also contribute to a more cohesive and motivated team, ultimately leading to improved organizational performance.

Implementing Win-Win Solutions

Implementing win-win solutions is a critical skill for managers and business leaders looking to foster collaboration and drive organizational success. A win-win approach ensures that all parties involved in a negotiation or conflict come away feeling satisfied with the outcome. This technique not only enhances relationships but also promotes a culture of trust and cooperation within teams. By focusing on mutual benefits, leaders can address underlying issues while ensuring that their own goals are met alongside those of their colleagues or clients.

To implement win-win solutions effectively, managers should start by actively listening to the concerns and interests of all stakeholders. This requires an open-minded approach where leaders set aside their assumptions and biases. By asking clarifying questions and encouraging dialogue, managers can uncover the underlying motivations of each party. This initial step is crucial, as it lays the groundwork for understanding how different perspectives can align to create a mutually beneficial solution.

Next, it is essential to approach problem-solving with creativity and flexibility. Managers should encourage brainstorming sessions where team members can propose various options that address the needs of all parties.

The emphasis should be on generating ideas rather than evaluating them initially. This open-ended approach can lead to innovative solutions that might not have been considered otherwise. By fostering a collaborative environment, leaders empower their teams to think outside the box and explore alternatives that serve everyone's interests.

Once potential solutions have been identified,

managers need to evaluate these options through a structured decision-making framework. This involves assessing how each solution aligns with the objectives of all parties involved. Leaders should encourage feedback and discussions about the feasibility and implications of each option. By involving stakeholders in the evaluation process, managers not only increase buy-in but also demonstrate that their input is valued, which is crucial for long-term engagement and commitment.

Finally, implementing the agreed-upon win- win solution requires clear communication and effective follow-up. Managers should articulate the details of the solution, ensuring that everyone understands their roles and responsibilities moving forward. Regular check-ins can help monitor progress and address any emerging concerns, reinforcing the collaborative spirit of the initial agreement. By maintaining open lines of communication, leaders can adjust the solution as needed, ensuring that it continues to meet the evolving needs of all parties involved. This ongoing commitment to collaboration will ultimately strengthen relationships and enhance the overall effectiveness of the team.

Chapter 13: Rapid Goal Setting and Prioritization

SMART Goals in a Nutshell

SMART goals offer a structured approach to setting objectives that are both clear and attainable. The acronym stands for Specific, Measurable, Achievable, Relevant, and Time-bound. This framework provides a comprehensive method for managers and business leaders to enhance their goal-setting processes. By utilizing SMART goals, leaders can ensure that their objectives are not only well-defined but also aligned with their organization's vision and mission, which is crucial for driving team performance and accountability.

Specificity is the first pillar of SMART goals. Goals should be clear and unambiguous, detailing exactly what needs to be accomplished. For instance, instead of stating a vague objective like "improve sales," a specific goal would be "increase sales by 20% in the Northeast region." This clarity helps team members understand the exact expectations and reduces the chances of confusion or misinterpretation. When goals are specific, they provide a clear direction for action and help focus efforts where they are most needed.

The second component, measurability, allows leaders to track progress and determine when a goal has been achieved. By establishing metrics or indicators, managers can assess performance quantitatively. For example, using sales figures or customer satisfaction ratings provides tangible evidence of progress. Measurable goals not only motivate teams by showing how far they've come but also enable leaders to make informed decisions based on real data, enhancing the overall effectiveness of the management process.

Achievability is crucial in ensuring that goals are realistic and attainable. While it is important to encourage teams to stretch their capabilities, setting unattainable goals can lead to frustration and disengagement.

Leaders must consider their team's resources, skills, and overall workload when setting goals. A well-balanced approach encourages ambition while maintaining morale. When teams believe their goals are achievable, they are more likely to commit fully to the effort required to accomplish them.

Relevance and time-bound elements round out the SMART framework. Goals must be pertinent to the organization's objectives and relevant to the team's work. This alignment ensures that employees see the value in their tasks, fostering a sense of purpose.

Additionally, time-bound goals create a sense of urgency and encourage timely completion. By setting deadlines, managers can maintain momentum and ensure that projects stay on track. Together, these elements of the SMART framework provide a powerful tool for managers to drive performance and foster a culture of accountability within their teams.

The 1-Page Goal Setting Worksheet

The 1-Page Goal Setting Worksheet is a practical

tool designed to streamline the goal-setting process for managers and business leaders. In an environment where time is often scarce, this worksheet allows leaders to focus their efforts on what truly matters. By condensing complex ideas into a single page, it provides clarity and direction, ensuring that both individual and team goals align with broader organizational objectives. This simplicity encourages quick reflection and prioritization, which are essential for effective leadership.

The worksheet is structured to facilitate the identification of SMART goals—Specific, Measurable, Achievable, Relevant, and Time-bound. Each section guides managers through the process of defining their goals succinctly. By focusing on these criteria, leaders can avoid vague aspirations and instead set clear targets that drive performance. This clarity not only enhances individual accountability but also fosters a sense of shared purpose among team members, as everyone understands the expectations and desired outcomes.

Additionally, the 1-Page Goal Setting Worksheet emphasizes the importance of regular review and adjustment. Managers are encouraged to revisit their goals periodically to assess progress and make necessary modifications. This practice is vital in today's fast-paced business landscape, where priorities can shift rapidly. By incorporating a review mechanism into the worksheet, leaders can remain agile, ensuring their goals stay relevant and aligned with the organization's evolving needs.

Another key feature of the worksheet is its focus on visualization. By allowing managers to map out their goals visually, it enhances comprehension and retention. Visual aids can serve as powerful reminders of what needs to be accomplished, making it easier for leaders to communicate their vision to their teams.

This shared visual understanding fosters collaboration, as team members can see how their individual contributions fit into the larger picture.

In conclusion, the 1-Page Goal Setting Worksheet is an invaluable resource for managers aiming to enhance their leadership effectiveness. Its straightforward design promotes rapid goal-setting and prioritization, ensuring that leaders can quickly adapt to changing circumstances. By utilizing this tool, managers not only clarify their own objectives but also empower their teams, ultimately driving better performance and achieving organizational success.

Prioritizing with the ABCD Method

The ABCD Method is a powerful tool for managers and business leaders seeking to enhance their prioritization skills and make effective decisions in a fast-paced environment. This method breaks down tasks into four distinct categories: A for "Must Do," B for "Should Do," C for "Could Do," and D for "Delegate or Drop." By categorizing tasks in this way, leaders can quickly assess what requires immediate attention and what can be postponed or assigned to others, ensuring that their focus remains on high-impact activities.

To implement the ABCD Method, start by listing all the tasks that need to be accomplished. Once you have a comprehensive list, analyze each task and assign it a letter based on its urgency and importance. Tasks categorized as "A" are those that are critical to achieving immediate goals and must be addressed first. These are often time-sensitive issues or projects that directly contribute to the organization's strategic objectives. By prioritizing these tasks, managers can ensure that they are addressing the most pressing needs of their team and organization.

Next, consider the "B" tasks, which are important but do not require immediate action. These tasks can be scheduled for later, allowing leaders to allocate time and resources accordingly. It's essential to keep these tasks visible on your agenda to ensure they are not neglected. "C" tasks are those that would be nice to accomplish but are not critical. These can often be postponed or integrated into the workflow as time permits. Finally, "D" tasks represent activities that can either be delegated to others or eliminated altogether. This process not only streamlines the workload but also empowers team members by involving them in tasks that align with their skills and expertise.

One of the significant advantages of the ABCD Method is its ability to foster a culture of accountability and collaboration. By defining which tasks can be delegated, managers encourage their teams to take ownership of responsibilities, enhancing engagement and productivity. This approach also allows business leaders to focus on strategic

decision-making and leadership, rather than getting bogged down in daily operational details. Regularly revisiting the ABCD framework can lead to continuous improvement in prioritization and time management.

In conclusion, the ABCD Method serves as an effective prioritization tool for busy managers and business leaders. By categorizing tasks based on urgency and importance, leaders can streamline their decision-making processes and focus on what truly matters. This method not only enhances individual productivity but also strengthens team dynamics, ultimately contributing to a more efficient and effective work environment. Embracing the ABCD Method can transform how you and your team approach daily challenges, leading to better outcomes and a more balanced workload.

Aligning Team Goals with Organizational Objectives

Aligning team goals with organizational objectives is essential for ensuring that every member of the team is working towards a common purpose. This alignment not only enhances productivity but also fosters a sense of ownership and accountability among team members. Managers can initiate this process by clearly communicating the organization's vision and mission. When team members understand how their work contributes to broader goals, they are more likely to feel motivated and engaged. Conducting regular meetings to discuss these objectives can help reinforce their importance and ensure that everyone is on the same page.

To effectively align team goals with organizational objectives, managers should involve team members in the goal-setting process. This collaborative approach not only garners buy-in but also encourages diverse perspectives, leading to more innovative solutions. Managers can facilitate brainstorming sessions where team members can share their insights on how their individual roles can contribute to the organization's goals. By incorporating input from the team, managers can create more relevant and achievable goals that resonate with each member's strengths and responsibilities.

Once the goals are established, it is crucial for managers to establish clear metrics for success. Defining key performance indicators (KPIs) allows both managers and team members to track progress and make necessary adjustments. These metrics should align with the organizational objectives, providing a roadmap for how the team will achieve its goals. Regularly reviewing these KPIs in team meetings can help maintain focus and accountability, ensuring that everyone remains aligned with the overall mission.

Furthermore, managers should implement a feedback loop to continuously assess the alignment between team goals and organizational objectives. This can be achieved through one-on-one check-ins, team retrospectives, or performance reviews. During these discussions, managers can identify any discrepancies and address challenges that may hinder progress. By being proactive in seeking feedback, managers can make timely adjustments to strategies and ensure that the team remains aligned with the organization's evolving objectives.

Finally, celebrating milestones and successes as a team can reinforce the importance of alignment. Recognizing achievements not only motivates team members but also reinforces the connection between their efforts and the organization's objectives.

Managers can create a culture of appreciation by acknowledging contributions that lead to the accomplishment of team goals. This recognition fosters a sense of belonging and encourages ongoing commitment to the organization's mission, ultimately leading to enhanced performance and a more cohesive team.

Chapter 14: Rapid Coaching Techniques

The Power of Brief Coaching Sessions

The concept of brief coaching sessions has gained significant traction in today's fast-paced business environment, where time is often a luxury that managers cannot afford. These sessions, typically lasting no more than a few minutes, can be highly effective in providing immediate support and guidance to team members. By leveraging brief coaching techniques, managers can address issues in real-time, foster a culture of continuous improvement, and enhance overall team performance without the burden of lengthy meetings.

One of the primary advantages of brief coaching sessions is their ability to facilitate quick decision-making. In moments when employees face challenges or uncertainties, a succinct coaching dialogue can help clarify their thought processes and illuminate possible solutions. By asking pointed questions and encouraging critical thinking, managers can empower their team members to arrive at decisions swiftly and confidently.

This not only accelerates progress but also instills a sense of ownership and accountability in employees, ultimately leading to a more dynamic work environment.

Additionally, brief coaching sessions serve as an effective tool for instant conflict resolution. Conflicts, whether interpersonal or task-related, can disrupt productivity and morale. By addressing conflicts promptly through focused coaching, managers can navigate tensions before they escalate. These sessions allow for open communication, enabling team members to express their concerns and collaboratively explore resolutions. This proactive approach not only mitigates the immediate issue but also fosters stronger relationships and a more cohesive team over time.

Rapid goal setting and prioritization are also enhanced through brief coaching techniques. Managers can use these sessions to help employees align their individual goals with broader organizational objectives. By facilitating quick discussions on priorities, managers can guide their teams in focusing on the most impactful tasks. This alignment not only boosts motivation but also ensures that everyone is working toward a common purpose, which is critical for achieving organizational success.

Finally, brief coaching sessions can be instrumental in providing efficient performance feedback. Instead of waiting for formal reviews, managers can deliver constructive feedback in real-time, allowing team members to make immediate adjustments. This ongoing feedback loop encourages continuous learning and development, ensuring that employees are consistently improving their skills and contributions. By integrating brief coaching into their leadership practices, managers can cultivate a more engaged and high- performing workforce, ultimately driving business success.

The GROW Model for Instant Guidance

The GROW model is a powerful framework for providing instant guidance to team members and enhancing their performance. It consists of four key components: Goal, Reality, Options, and Will. This structured approach enables managers to facilitate effective conversations that lead to actionable outcomes in a time-efficient manner. By utilizing the GROW model, managers can help their teams clarify their objectives, assess their current situations, explore potential solutions, and commit to actionable steps, all within a concise timeframe.

Beginning with the Goal component, managers encourage team members to define clear, specific, and measurable objectives. This step is crucial as it sets the direction for the conversation and ensures everyone is aligned on the desired outcomes. Effective leaders ask probing questions that prompt individuals to articulate what they want to achieve, fostering a sense of ownership and motivation. By keeping goals focused and attainable, managers can inspire their teams to work diligently toward success.

The next phase, Reality, involves an honest assessment of the current situation. Here, managers guide their team members to identify any existing obstacles, resources, and challenges that may hinder progress. This step requires open dialogue and active listening, allowing managers to gain insight into their team's perspectives. Addressing reality helps to ground the discussion in practical terms, ensuring that the team understands where they currently stand in relation to their goals and what adjustments may be necessary to move forward.

Once the current reality is established, the Options phase prompts exploration of various strategies and solutions. Managers can facilitate brainstorming sessions where team members collaboratively consider multiple avenues for achieving their goals. This encourages creativity and innovation, leading to a richer pool of ideas. By guiding the discussion towards evaluating the pros and cons of each option, managers can help their teams make informed decisions about the best paths forward, building confidence and engagement in the process.

Finally, the Will component is where commitment is solidified. Managers assist their team members in articulating specific actions they will take, along with timelines for accountability. This phase often involves setting up follow-up discussions to review progress and adjust plans as necessary. By reinforcing commitment, managers ensure that the insights gained from the GROW model translate into tangible results. Overall, the GROW model serves as a rapid, effective tool for managers to provide guidance, foster development, and drive team performance in a busy work environment.

Effective Questioning Techniques

As a manager or business leader, the ability to ask effective questions is fundamental to fostering communication and collaboration within your team. Questions are not merely tools for gathering information; they are powerful instruments for guiding discussions, encouraging critical thinking, and driving engagement. By mastering effective questioning techniques, you can create a dynamic environment that promotes problem solving and innovation.

One essential technique is to use open-ended questions. These questions invite team members to elaborate on their thoughts, encouraging deeper insights and a broader perspective. Instead of asking, "Did you complete the project?" consider asking, "What challenges did you face during the project, and how did you overcome them?" This approach not only provides you with valuable information but also empowers employees to reflect on their experiences and share their learning.

Another effective technique is to employ probing questions to dig deeper into a topic. Probing questions help clarify ideas and challenge assumptions, leading to more thorough discussions. For example, if a team member presents an idea, you might ask, "What evidence do you have to support this approach?" or "How does this align with our overall strategy?" By using probing questions, you encourage critical thinking and ensure that decisions are based on solid reasoning.

Additionally, incorporating reflective questions can enhance team dynamics and personal growth. Reflective questions prompt individuals to think about their experiences and behaviors, fostering self-awareness. Asking questions like, "What did you learn from this situation?" or "How could we approach this differently next time?" encourages team members to evaluate their performance and embrace a culture of continuous improvement.

Lastly, timing and context are crucial when utilizing questioning techniques. Be mindful of when and how you pose questions to create an open atmosphere conducive to discussion. During team meetings, consider incorporating a round of questions after presenting a new initiative or during brainstorming sessions to facilitate participation. By strategically using questioning techniques, you not only enhance communication but also drive your team toward greater clarity, accountability, and success.

Celebrating Small Wins

Celebrating small wins is a crucial aspect of effective leadership that often goes overlooked. In a fast-paced business environment, managers tend to focus on larger goals and milestones, neglecting the importance of recognizing incremental achievements. This oversight can lead to decreased morale and motivation among team members. By implementing a strategy for celebrating small wins, managers can foster a positive work culture that encourages continuous progress and engagement.

Recognizing small victories can significantly enhance team motivation. When team members receive acknowledgment for their contributions, no matter how minor, it reinforces their sense of purpose and belonging within the organization. This recognition can take many forms, from a simple verbal acknowledgment during a meeting to a more structured reward system. The key is to ensure that these celebrations are genuine and timely, which helps to create an environment where employees feel valued for their efforts.

Incorporating small win celebrations into regular

team meetings can be an effective technique for managers. By dedicating a few moments at the start or end of a meeting to highlight recent achievements, leaders can create a culture of appreciation. This practice not only boosts morale but also encourages transparency and collaboration. Team members are more likely to share their successes and challenges, fostering a supportive atmosphere where everyone feels empowered to contribute to collective goals.

Moreover, celebrating small wins can serve as a powerful tool for maintaining momentum in long-term projects. Large objectives can often seem daunting and may lead to feelings of overwhelm among team members. By breaking these objectives down into smaller, manageable tasks and celebrating each completion, managers can help their teams maintain focus and energy. This approach not only keeps projects on track but also instills a sense of accomplishment that propels teams forward.

Finally, it is essential for managers to model the behavior they wish to see in their teams. By openly celebrating their own small wins and encouraging others to do the same, leaders can demonstrate the importance of recognizing progress at every level. This practice cultivates a growth mindset within the organization, where continuous improvement is valued and celebrated.

Ultimately, the habit of acknowledging small wins can transform a team's culture, leading to increased engagement, productivity, and overall satisfaction in the workplace.

Chapter 15: Efficient Performance Feedback Methods

Delivering Feedback in Under a Minute

Delivering feedback effectively and efficiently is a critical skill for managers and business leaders. In today's fast-paced business environment, where time is often limited, being able to provide constructive feedback in under a minute can significantly enhance team performance and morale. The key to this rapid feedback approach lies in clarity and focus. By distilling feedback to its essential elements, you can convey meaningful insights without overwhelming your team members.

To deliver feedback quickly, start by identifying the core message you want to communicate. Focus on one specific behavior or outcome that needs addressing, rather than trying to cover multiple points at once. This clarity allows you to articulate your thoughts succinctly and ensures that the recipient understands the primary focus of your feedback. Use straightforward language and avoid jargon to prevent misunderstandings and to keep the conversation accessible.

Incorporating the "sandwich" method can also be effective in brief feedback sessions. Begin with a positive remark to set a constructive tone, followed by the area for improvement, and conclude with another positive note or encouragement. This technique not only softens the impact of the critique but also reinforces the recipient's strengths, fostering a positive atmosphere despite the necessary corrections. Ensure that each part of the sandwich is concise to maintain the one- minute timeframe.

Timing is crucial when delivering feedback. Choose appropriate moments to provide feedback, such as immediately after a relevant event or during a scheduled one-on-one meeting. This immediacy helps the feedback resonate more with the individual, as the context is fresh in their mind. Additionally, be mindful of your body language and tone, as nonverbal cues play a significant role in how feedback is received. A friendly demeanor can help create an open environment where the recipient feels comfortable receiving and processing the information.

Finally, encourage a two-way dialogue by inviting responses or questions after your feedback. This interaction not only clarifies any misunderstandings but also empowers team members to take ownership of their development. By fostering a culture of open communication, you enhance engagement and reinforce the value of feedback within your team. Managers who master the art of delivering feedback efficiently contribute to a more dynamic and responsive workplace, ultimately driving better performance and satisfaction among their teams.

The Sandwich Method Explained

The Sandwich Method is a powerful communication technique that enhances the delivery of feedback, making it more palatable for the recipient while ensuring the message is conveyed effectively. This method involves structuring feedback by placing a critical comment between two positive remarks. For busy managers and business leaders, this approach not only aids in maintaining morale but also fosters a more receptive environment for constructive criticism. By employing the Sandwich Method, you can ensure that your feedback is both effective and encouraging, promoting a culture of continuous improvement within your team.

To implement the Sandwich Method, start with a genuine positive observation about the individual's performance or contributions. This initial praise sets a constructive tone and prepares the recipient to receive further feedback. It's essential that this compliment is sincere and specific, as vague praise can diminish its effectiveness. For instance, instead of saying, "You did a good job," you could say, "Your presentation was well-organized and engaging, which kept the audience's attention." This approach not only boosts the recipient's confidence but also reinforces the behaviors you want to encourage.

Following the positive remark, introduce the critical feedback. It is crucial to be clear and specific about the areas that need improvement. This part of the Sandwich Method should focus on behaviors, not personal attributes. For example, instead of saying, "You're not a good team player," you might say, "I noticed there were instances during the project where you chose to work independently rather than collaborating with the team." This phrasing maintains respect and objectivity, making it easier for the recipient to accept and understand the feedback.

After addressing the critical feedback, it is time to conclude with another positive remark. This final layer is important as it leaves the recipient with a sense of encouragement and motivation. It can be a reaffirmation of their strengths or a statement about your confidence in their ability to improve. For example, you might say, "I appreciate your dedication and creativity, and I believe that by working more collaboratively, you will enhance your already impressive contributions." This closing helps to reinforce the relationship and encourages a proactive approach to personal development.

The Sandwich Method, when applied correctly, can

lead to more effective communication and stronger team dynamics. Managers who consistently utilize this technique can create an environment where feedback is viewed as a tool for growth rather than criticism. By framing discussions in a constructive manner, leaders can enhance team performance, foster open communication, and build trust, all of which are essential elements of effective leadership. Implementing this method into your regular feedback sessions can transform the way your team approaches challenges and personal development, ultimately driving better outcomes for your organization.

Utilizing Peer Feedback for Growth

Utilizing peer feedback for growth is a strategic approach that can significantly enhance team performance and individual development. For managers and business leaders, fostering an environment where constructive feedback is regularly exchanged among peers can lead to a more engaged workforce. Peer feedback not only empowers employees to take ownership of their growth but also cultivates a culture of collaboration and continuous improvement. By integrating structured feedback mechanisms, leaders can encourage open dialogue, which is essential for identifying strengths and areas for development.

To effectively implement peer feedback, managers should initiate regular feedback sessions that are structured and focused. These sessions can take the form of informal check-ins or more formalized review processes. Encouraging employees to share their insights on each other's performance helps create a sense of accountability and mutual respect. It is crucial for leaders to model this behavior by actively seeking feedback from their peers and demonstrating how to accept it graciously. This helps to normalize the practice and reduces any apprehension team members may have regarding giving or receiving feedback.

Incorporating tools such as peer review forms or feedback apps can streamline the process, making it more efficient and less time-consuming. These tools can guide employees in providing specific, actionable feedback rather than vague comments.

Additionally, offering training on how to deliver and receive feedback constructively can equip team members with the skills they need to engage in meaningful conversations. Managers should emphasize the importance of focusing on behaviors and outcomes instead of personal traits, which can help maintain a positive atmosphere during feedback exchanges.

The benefits of utilizing peer feedback extend beyond individual growth; they also contribute to team cohesion and improved performance. When employees feel supported by their colleagues, they are more likely to take risks and innovate. This collaborative environment leads to enhanced problem-solving as team members leverage each other's strengths.

Furthermore, peer feedback can serve as a catalyst for identifying training needs within the team, allowing managers to tailor development programs that align with the specific requirements of their workforce.

Ultimately, fostering a culture of peer feedback is a

powerful tool for managers looking to enhance their leadership effectiveness. By prioritizing and facilitating regular feedback exchanges, leaders can create a dynamic workplace where employees are motivated to grow and excel. This not only leads to improved individual performance but also drives overall organizational success. Managers who embrace this practice position themselves as champions of development, empowering their teams to reach their full potential.

Creating a Feedback Culture

Creating a feedback culture within an organization is essential for fostering an environment of continuous improvement and engagement. To start, managers must understand that feedback should be a two-way street. Employees should feel encouraged to share their thoughts and insights, not just receive evaluations from their superiors. This open communication channel helps to build trust and transparency, which are critical components of a thriving workplace.

Implementing regular feedback sessions, where both managers and employees can express their views, can significantly enhance the overall morale and performance of the team.

One effective method to cultivate this culture is through the establishment of structured feedback processes. Managers can introduce routine check-ins, where constructive feedback is given and received in a safe and supportive setting. These sessions should be brief but impactful, focusing on specific behaviors or outcomes rather than general traits. By keeping feedback focused and actionable, employees are more likely to feel motivated to improve and contribute positively to the organization's goals.

Additionally, integrating feedback into daily operations can normalize its importance.

Managers can encourage their teams to give each other feedback regularly, perhaps through peer review systems or informal conversations. This not only enhances collaboration but also empowers employees to take ownership of their development.

Acknowledging and celebrating instances where team members successfully implement feedback reinforces the idea that growth is a collective effort, further embedding this practice into the organization's culture.

Training managers on effective feedback techniques is equally vital. Leaders should be equipped with the skills to deliver feedback that is not only constructive but also empathetic. Workshops and role-playing scenarios can help managers practice these techniques, enabling them to approach conversations with confidence and clarity. By modeling effective feedback behavior, managers set the tone for their teams, demonstrating that feedback is a valuable tool for personal and professional growth.

Lastly, measuring the impact of feedback initiatives is crucial. Managers should regularly assess how feedback is received and utilized within their teams, adjusting their strategies as necessary. Surveys or informal discussions can provide insights into employees' perceptions of the feedback culture. By continuously refining their approach based on these assessments, managers can ensure that feedback remains a dynamic and integral part of their organizational culture, ultimately driving engagement and performance to new heights.

Chapter 16: Simple Change Management Approaches

The Need for Change in Business

The business landscape is evolving at an unprecedented pace, driven by technological advancements, shifting consumer expectations, and global competition.

Managers and business leaders must recognize that the need for change is not merely a reaction to external pressures but a proactive strategy for sustained growth and relevance. Embracing change enables organizations to innovate, improve efficiency, and enhance customer satisfaction. Without a willingness to adapt, businesses risk stagnation and may ultimately lose their competitive edge.

One of the core reasons for initiating change within a business is the necessity to align with market demands. Consumer preferences are continuously shifting, influenced by trends and emerging technologies. Managers need to stay attuned to these changes to ensure their products and services meet evolving expectations. This requires not only understanding market research but also being agile in the decision-making process. Quick decision-making frameworks can be implemented to assess when to pivot strategies or adjust offerings, ensuring that businesses remain attuned to their customer base.

Additionally, internal factors such as employee engagement and organizational culture play a critical role in the need for change. A disengaged workforce can lead to decreased productivity and high turnover rates, which ultimately impact the bottom line. Managers must adopt efficient performance feedback methods to foster a culture of open communication and continuous improvement. By providing rapid feedback and recognizing contributions, leaders can motivate employees to embrace change as a shared goal, rather than a top-down mandate.

Conflict is an inevitable part of any organization, particularly during periods of change. Managers equipped with instant conflict resolution tactics can navigate these challenges effectively. Addressing disputes promptly and constructively not only resolves issues but also builds trust within teams, creating an environment conducive to collaboration and innovation. When employees feel their concerns are acknowledged and addressed, they are more likely to support change initiatives.

Finally, the implementation of simple change management approaches is essential for ensuring that transitions are smooth and effective. Rapid goal setting and prioritization techniques enable leaders to break down complex changes into manageable steps, making the process less daunting for teams. By framing change as a series of achievable objectives, managers can foster a sense of progress and accomplishment. This approach not only facilitates adaptation but also reinforces the idea that change is a continuous journey rather than a one-time event, encouraging a culture of ongoing improvement and resilience within the organization.

The ADKAR Model Simplified

The ADKAR model, developed by Prosci, offers a straightforward framework for managing change effectively within organizations. It focuses on five key elements: Awareness, Desire, Knowledge, Ability, and Reinforcement. By breaking down the change process into these manageable components, managers can facilitate smoother transitions and enhance employee engagement. This simplified approach allows leaders to address each element systematically, ensuring that every team member is aligned with the change initiative.

Awareness is the first step in the ADKAR model, emphasizing the importance of communicating why the change is necessary. For busy managers, this means crafting clear and concise messages that resonate with employees. Utilize team meetings, emails, and informal conversations to convey the reasons behind the change. Highlighting the benefits and potential impacts on the team can foster an environment of understanding and reduce resistance. When employees grasp the rationale, they are more likely to support the change.

The second element, Desire, involves cultivating a genuine interest in the change among team members. Managers can encourage this by actively involving employees in the decision-making process, seeking their input, and addressing their concerns. Creating a culture of openness and trust enables leaders to tap into employees' intrinsic motivation. Recognizing individual contributions and aligning the change with personal and professional goals can further enhance this desire, making employees feel valued and invested in the transition.

Knowledge, the third component, refers to equipping employees with the necessary information and skills to adapt to the change. Managers should assess the current skill gaps and provide targeted training sessions, resources, or mentorship opportunities. This could involve quick workshops, online modules, or one-on-one coaching, depending on the complexity of the change. Providing accessible knowledge not only boosts confidence but also prepares employees to tackle new challenges effectively.

Ability, the fourth element, is about ensuring that

employees can implement the change successfully. This requires ongoing support and encouragement from management.

Implementing pilot programs or phased rollouts can help assess employee readiness and address any obstacles that arise.

Feedback mechanisms, such as regular check-ins or surveys, allow managers to gauge progress and make necessary adjustments. By demonstrating commitment to their success, leaders can reinforce the importance of the change and foster a culture of adaptability.

Finally, Reinforcement solidifies the change within the organizational culture. Managers should celebrate achievements, both big and small, to maintain momentum and motivate employees. Recognition programs, team celebrations, and performance reviews that highlight the positive outcomes of the change can strengthen commitment. Additionally, establishing accountability measures ensures that the change is sustained over time. By embedding these practices into the daily operations, leaders can create a resilient organization that thrives on continuous improvement and embraces future changes with confidence.

Communicating Change Effectively

Communicating change effectively is a critical skill for managers and business leaders, especially in today's fast-paced work environment. Change can often be met with resistance, fear, or confusion among team members. To mitigate these reactions, it is essential to communicate the reasons behind the change clearly and consistently. Start by outlining the vision for the change, explaining why it is necessary, and how it aligns with the organization's goals. This foundational step helps to create a shared understanding and buy-in from team members, making them more receptive to the transition.

Utilizing various communication channels can enhance the effectiveness of your message. Tailor your approach to fit the preferences of your team, whether that means face-to-face meetings, email updates, or team briefings. Ensure that the message is accessible and engaging, incorporating visuals or anecdotes if applicable. Additionally, encourage two-way communication by inviting feedback and questions from your team. This not only clarifies any misunderstandings but also empowers employees, making them feel valued and involved in the change process.

Consistency is key when communicating change. Regular updates should be provided throughout the transition, reinforcing the message and addressing any emerging concerns. Establishing a communication schedule helps maintain momentum and keeps the team informed about progress and next steps. It is also beneficial to highlight successes and milestones achieved during the change process. Celebrating small wins fosters a positive atmosphere and motivates the team to stay engaged.

Understanding the emotional impact of change is vital. Acknowledge that team members may experience anxiety or uncertainty during transitions. Take the time to empathize with their feelings and provide reassurance. Share resources such as training sessions or support groups to help ease the transition. By validating their concerns and offering support, you create a culture of trust and resilience, which can ultimately lead to a smoother implementation of change.

Finally, measuring the effectiveness of your communication and the change process itself is essential for continuous improvement.

Gather feedback through surveys, one-on-one conversations, or team discussions to assess how well the change has been communicated and received. Analyze this data to identify areas for improvement and adjust your strategies accordingly. By remaining adaptable and responsive, you not only enhance your communication skills but also foster a more agile and engaged workforce ready to embrace future changes.

Engaging Teams in the Change Process

Engaging teams in the change process is crucial for the successful implementation of new strategies and initiatives. When managers actively involve their team members, they foster a sense of ownership and accountability that can significantly enhance morale and productivity. To begin this engagement, it is essential to clearly communicate the reasons behind the change. This involves sharing the vision, goals, and expected outcomes, which allows team members to understand not only what is changing but also why it is necessary.

Utilizing clear and concise language ensures that everyone is on the same page, reducing potential misunderstandings that can arise during transitional periods.

Once the purpose of the change is established, incorporating team members into the planning and execution phases is vital. This can be achieved through brainstorming sessions, surveys, or focus groups that solicit feedback and ideas. By doing so, managers not only gather valuable insights but also demonstrate that they value their employees' perspectives. This collaborative approach can lead to innovative solutions that management may not have considered. Furthermore, involving team members in decision-making fosters a sense of empowerment, which can enhance their commitment to the change process.

Training and resources are essential components when engaging teams in change. Providing team members with the necessary tools and knowledge will equip them to adapt more effectively. This may include workshops, seminars, or access to online learning platforms that address the specific skills needed for the change initiative. Regular check-ins during the training process can help monitor progress and address any challenges team members may face.

Managers should also encourage peer support, enabling employees to learn from one another and share best practices, thus creating a culture of continuous improvement.

Recognizing and celebrating milestones throughout

the change process is another powerful way to maintain team engagement. Acknowledging both individual and team achievements fosters motivation and reinforces the idea that their contributions are valued. Simple gestures such as shout-outs during team meetings or small rewards can significantly boost morale. Additionally, creating opportunities for team members to share their experiences and successes can further build a sense of community and shared purpose, turning the change process into a collective effort.

Lastly, ongoing communication during and after the change is essential for sustaining engagement. Managers must be transparent about challenges and successes as the change unfolds. This not only keeps everyone informed but also allows for adjustments and improvements based on real-time feedback. Regularly scheduled meetings or updates can facilitate this ongoing dialogue, ensuring that team members feel supported throughout the transition. By maintaining open lines of communication, managers can reinforce trust and collaboration, ultimately leading to a more resilient and adaptable team.

About the Author:

Linda Thornton is a leading business expert and high performing team builder, blending her extensive academic background with real-world business acumen. With a degree in Business Administration from Harvard University, she has spent over two decades helping organizations transform their sales approach. Known for her innovative methods and engaging style, Linda Thornton has been a sought-after keynote speaker at international conferences and a trusted advisor to Fortune 500 companies. Her groundbreaking book, <u>The Art of Consultative Selling: Strategies for Lasting Relationships</u>, reflects her deep commitment to fostering meaningful connections and driving sustainable business growth. When she's not writing or speaking, Linda Thornton enjoys mentoring young professionals.

www.ingramcontent.com/pod-product-compliance
Lightning Source LLC
Chambersburg PA
CBHW052255220526
45471CB00001B/341